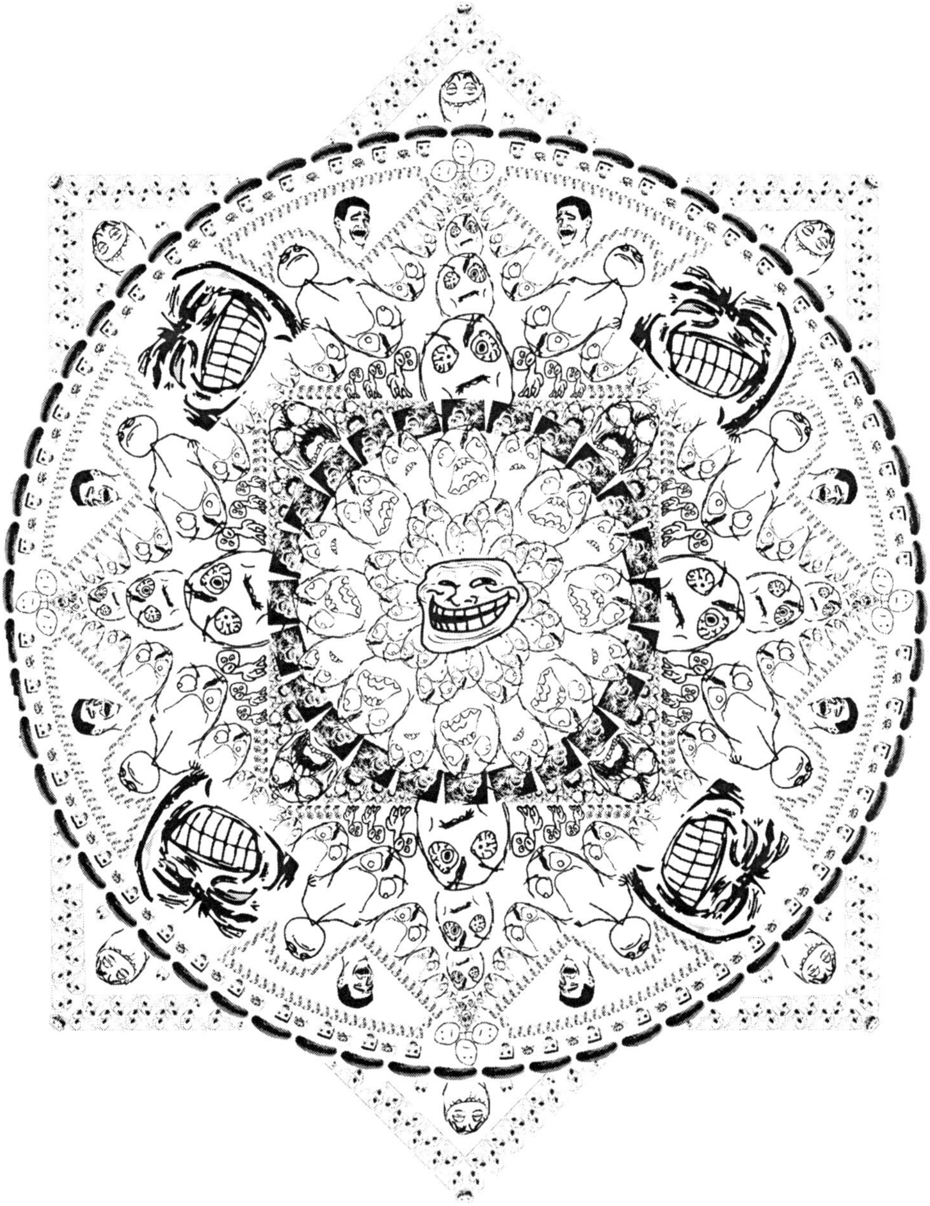

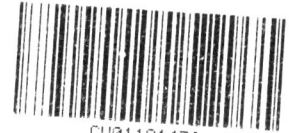

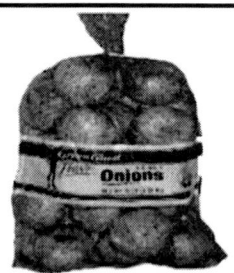

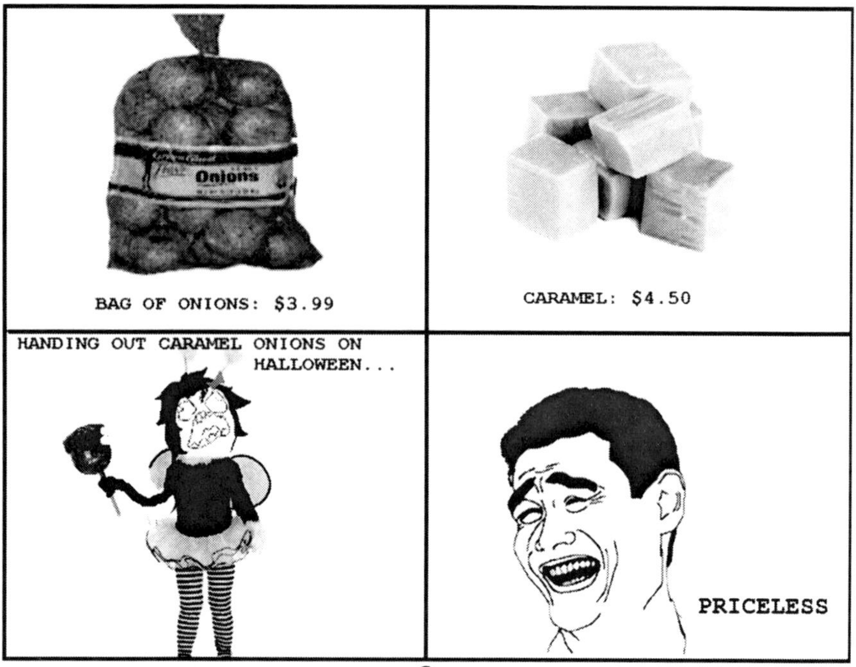
BAG OF ONIONS: $3.99
CARAMEL: $4.50
HANDING OUT CARAMEL ONIONS ON HALLOWEEN...
PRICELESS

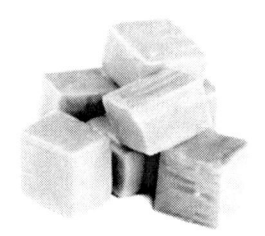

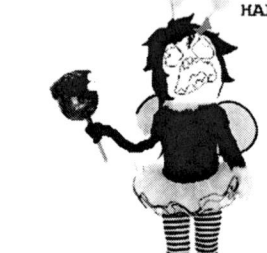

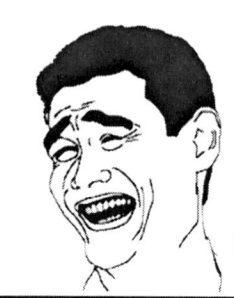

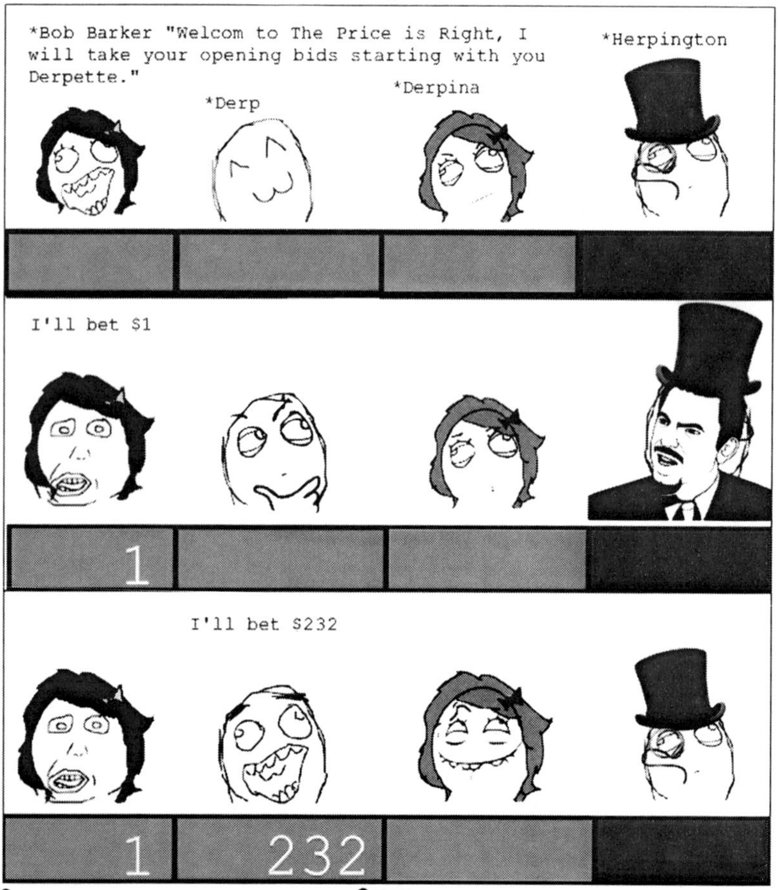
*Bob Barker "Welcom to The Price is Right, I will take your opening bids starting with you Derpette."
*Derp
*Derpina
*Herpington
I'll bet $1
1
I'll bet $232
1
232

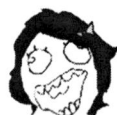

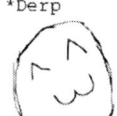

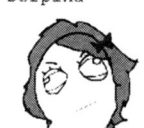

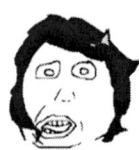

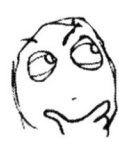

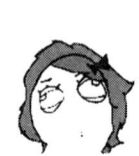

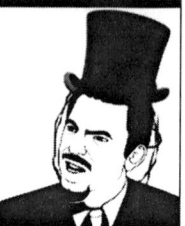

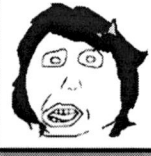

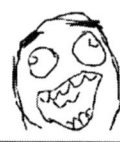

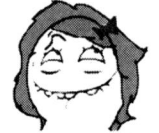

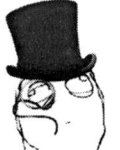

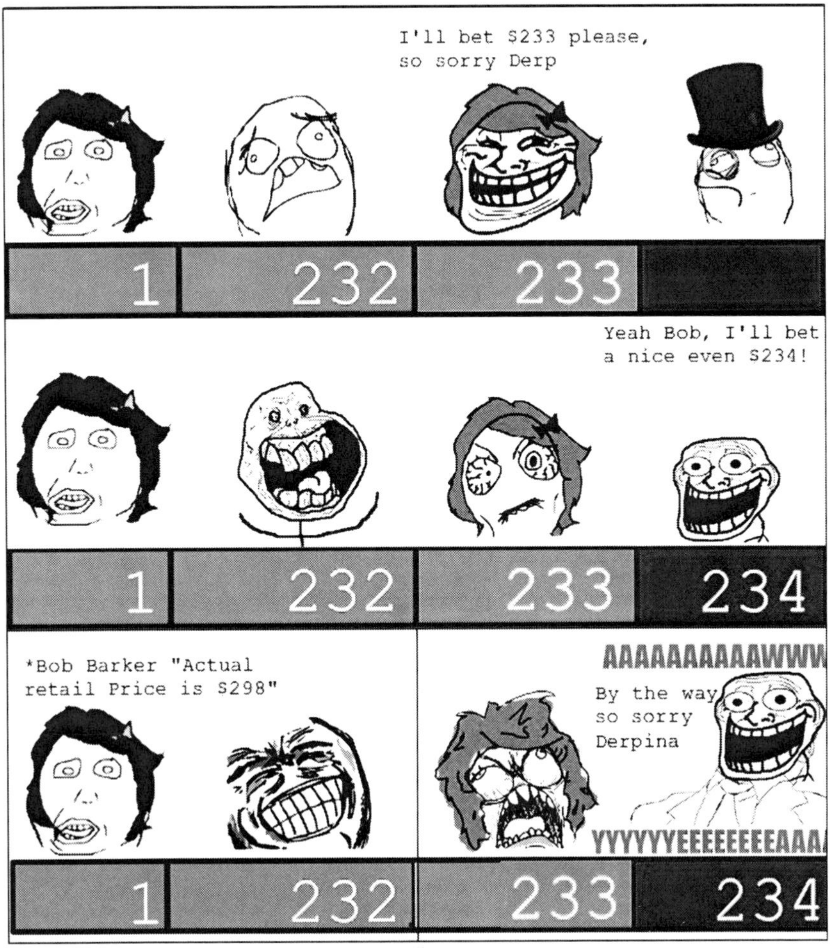
I'll bet $233 please,
so sorry Derp
1
232
233
Yeah Bob, I'll bet
a nice even $234!
1
232
233
234
*Bob Barker "Actual
retail Price is $298"
AAAAAAAAAWWW
By the way
so sorry
Derpina
YYYYYYEEEEEEEEAAAA
1
232
233
234

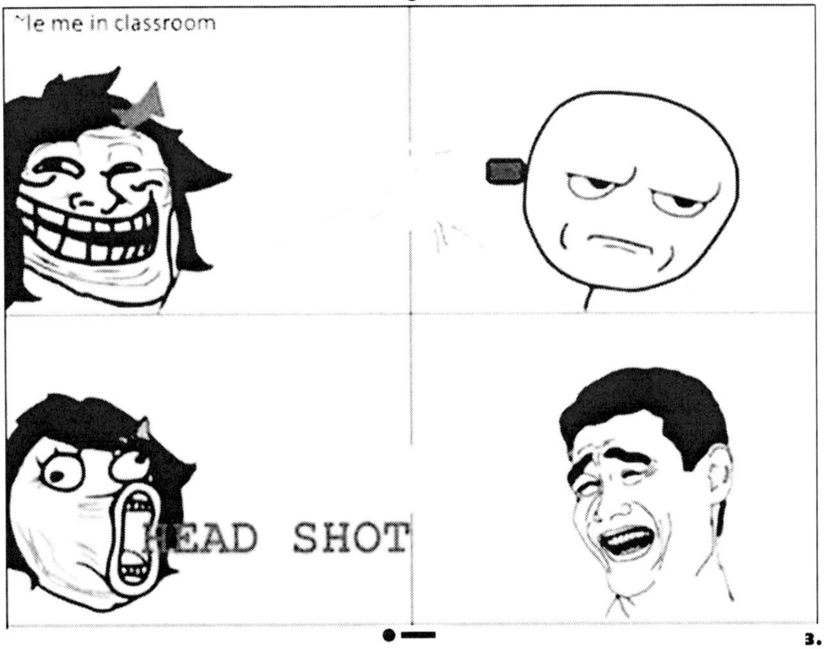
le me in classroom
HEAD SHOT

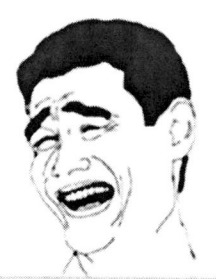
 FACEBOOK

le me, weed eating for near minimum wage to pay off student loans

"This sucks! It's hot and itchy! I'm tired! Herp derp!"

"I hate this! Who has ever been successful cutting grass for chump change?"

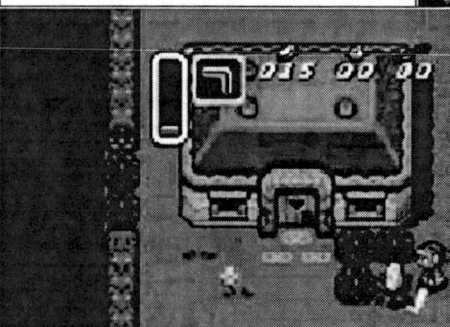
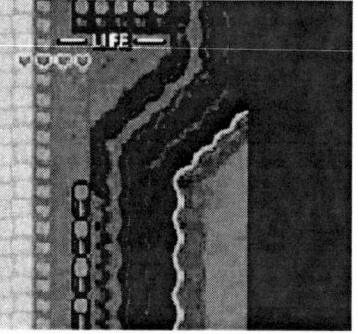

I AM THE CHOSEN ONE.

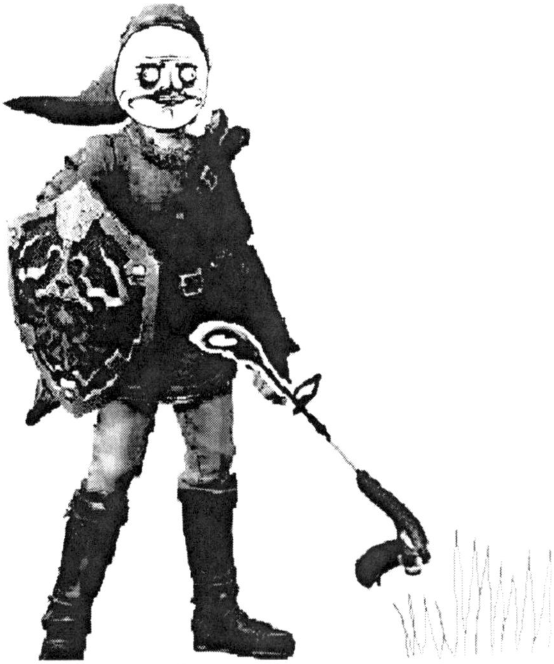

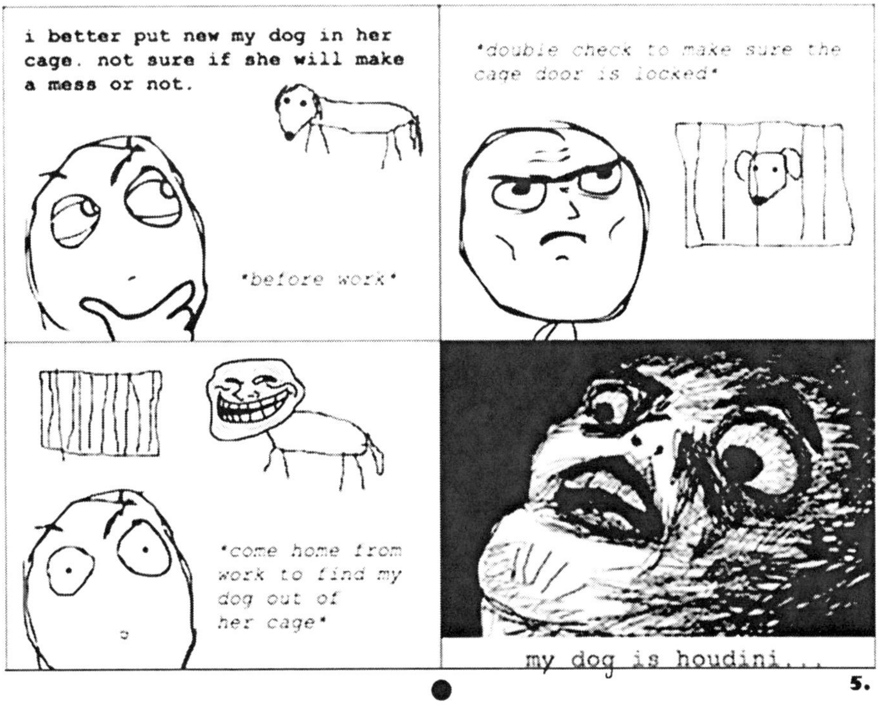
i better put new my dog in her cage. not sure if she will make a mess or not.
before work
double check to make sure the cage door is locked
come home from work to find my dog out of her cage
my dog is houdini...

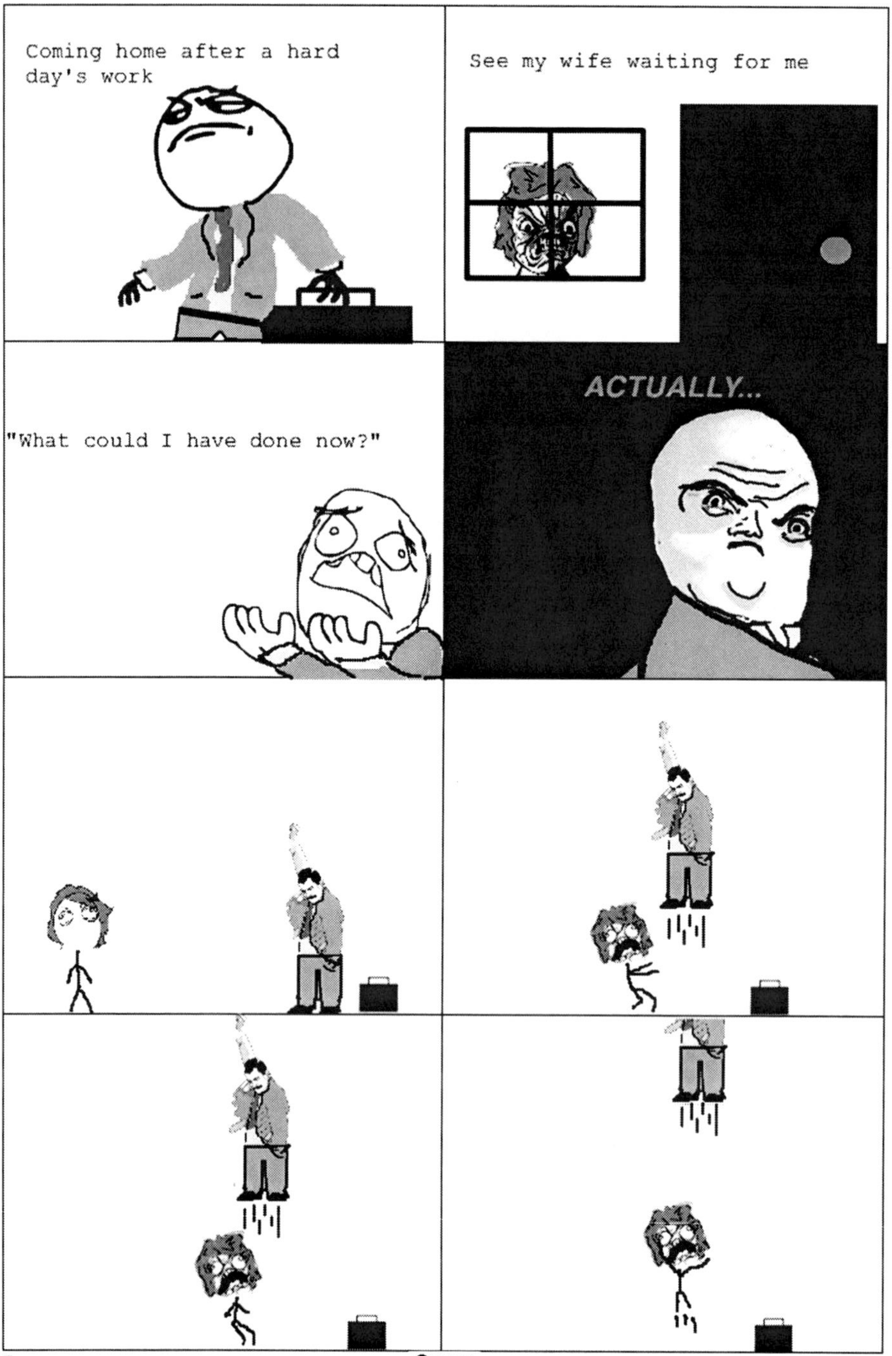
Coming home after a hard day's work
See my wife waiting for me
"What could I have done now?"
ACTUALLY...

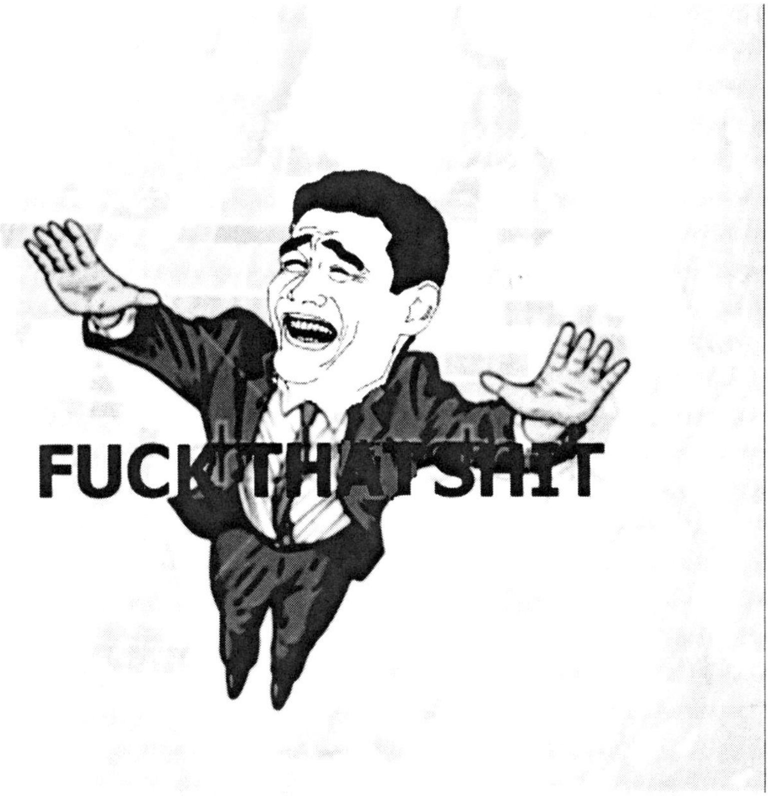
FUCK THAT SHIT

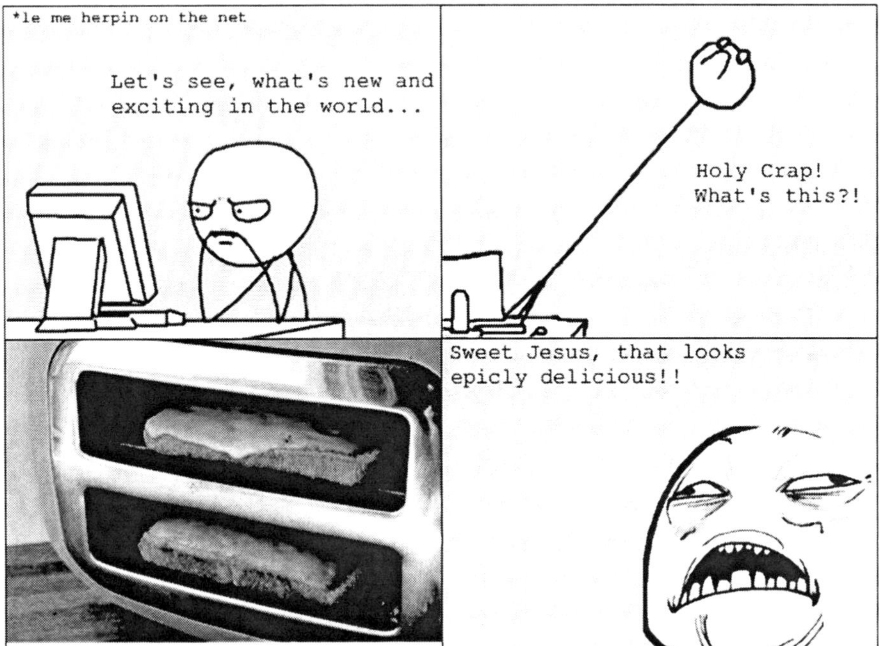
*le me herpin on the net
Let's see, what's new and exciting in the world...
Holy Crap! What's this?!
Turn toaster sideways, get grilled cheese.
Sweet Jesus, that looks epicly delicious!!

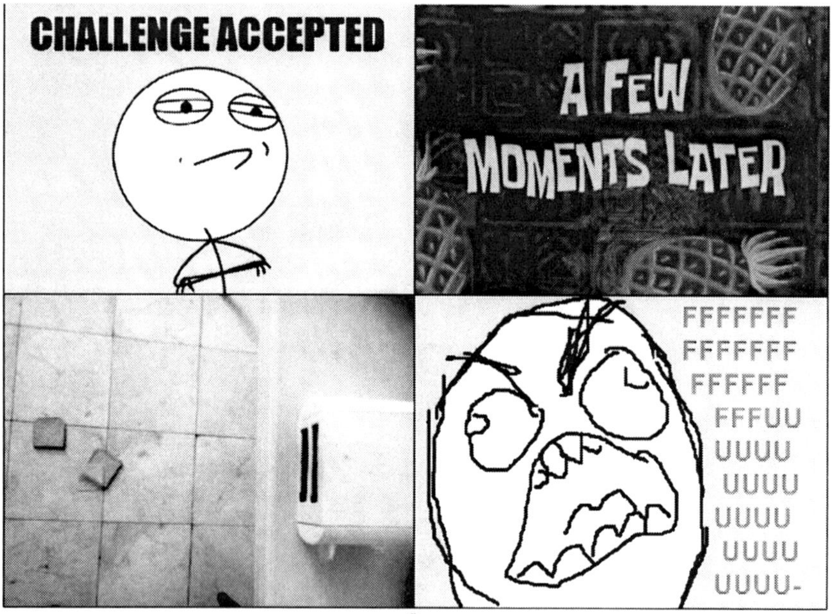
CHALLENGE ACCEPTED
A FEW MOMENTS LATER
FFFFFFF
FFFFFFF
FFFFFF
FFFUU
UUUU
UUUU
UUUU
UUUU
UUUU-

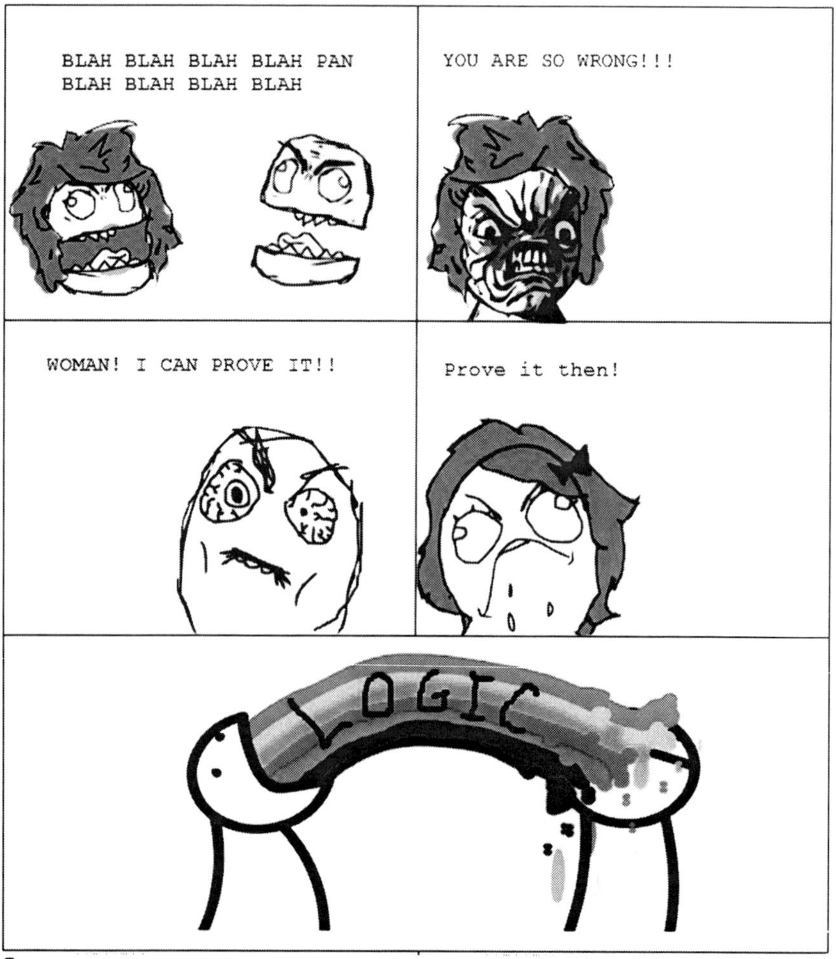
BLAH BLAH BLAH BLAH PAN BLAH BLAH BLAH BLAH
YOU ARE SO WRONG!!!
WOMAN! I CAN PROVE IT!!
Prove it then!
LOGIC

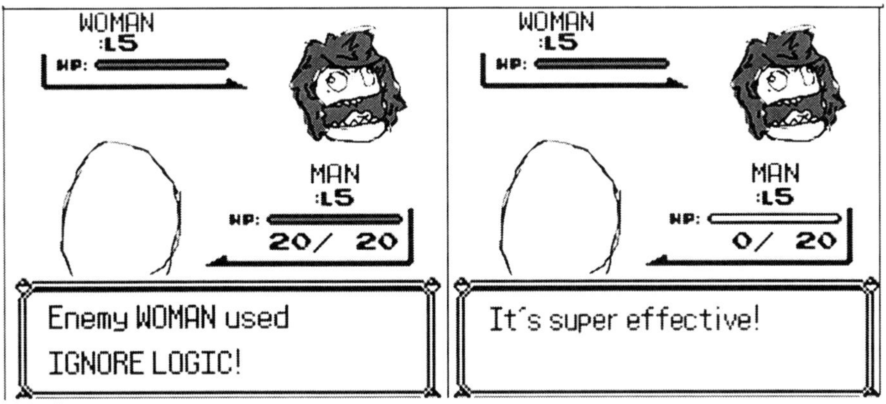
WOMAN
:L5
HP:
MAN
:L5
HP:
20/ 20
Enemy WOMAN used
IGNORE LOGIC!
WOMAN
:L5
HP:
MAN
:L5
HP:
0/ 20
It´s super effective!

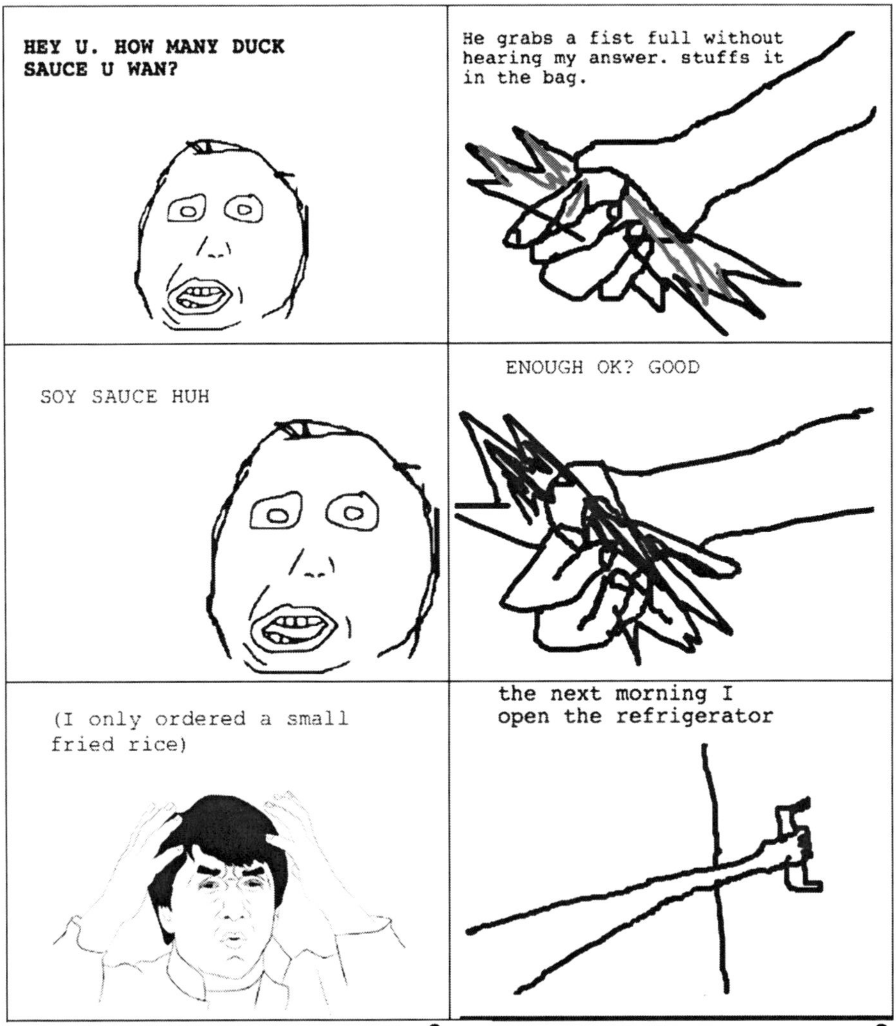
HEY U. HOW MANY DUCK SAUCE U WAN?
He grabs a fist full without hearing my answer. stuffs it in the bag.
SOY SAUCE HUH
ENOUGH OK? GOOD
(I only ordered a small fried rice)
the next morning I open the refrigerator

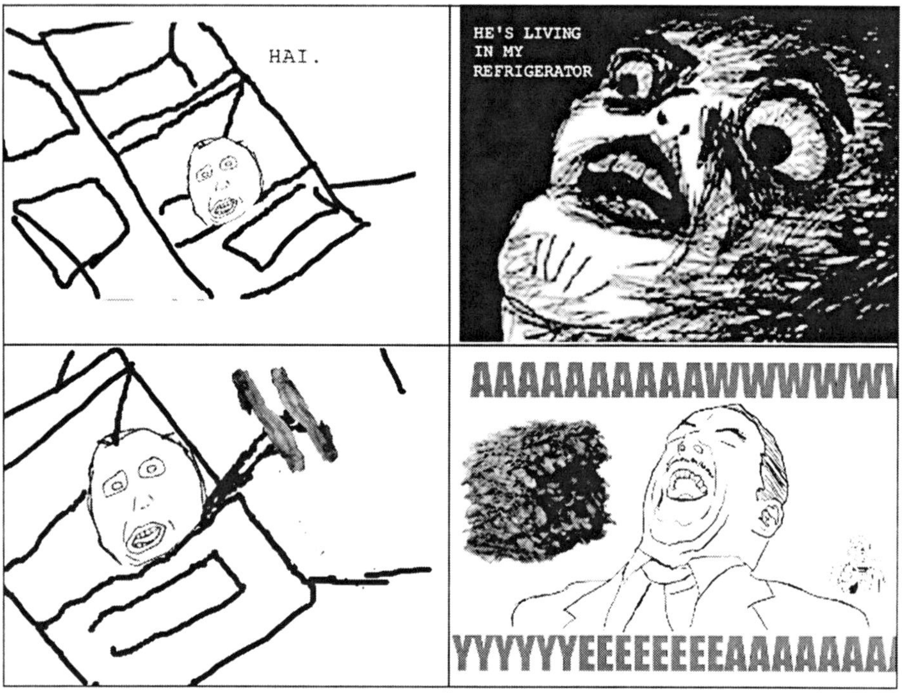
HAI.
HE'S LIVING IN MY REFRIGERATOR
AAAAAAAAAWWWWW
YYYYYEEEEEEEEAAAAAAA

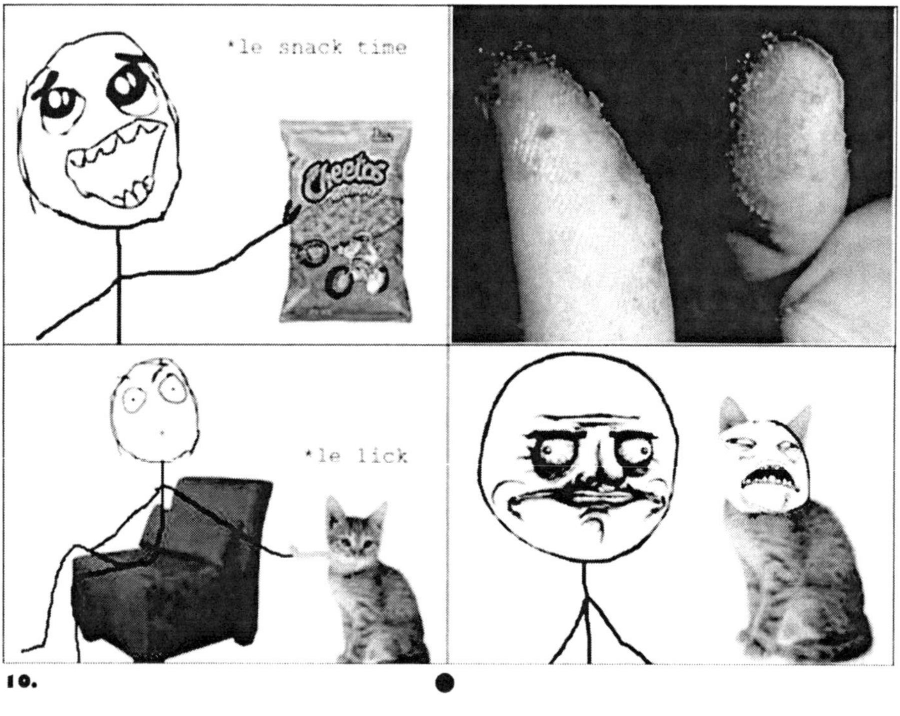
*le snack time
Cheetos
*le lick

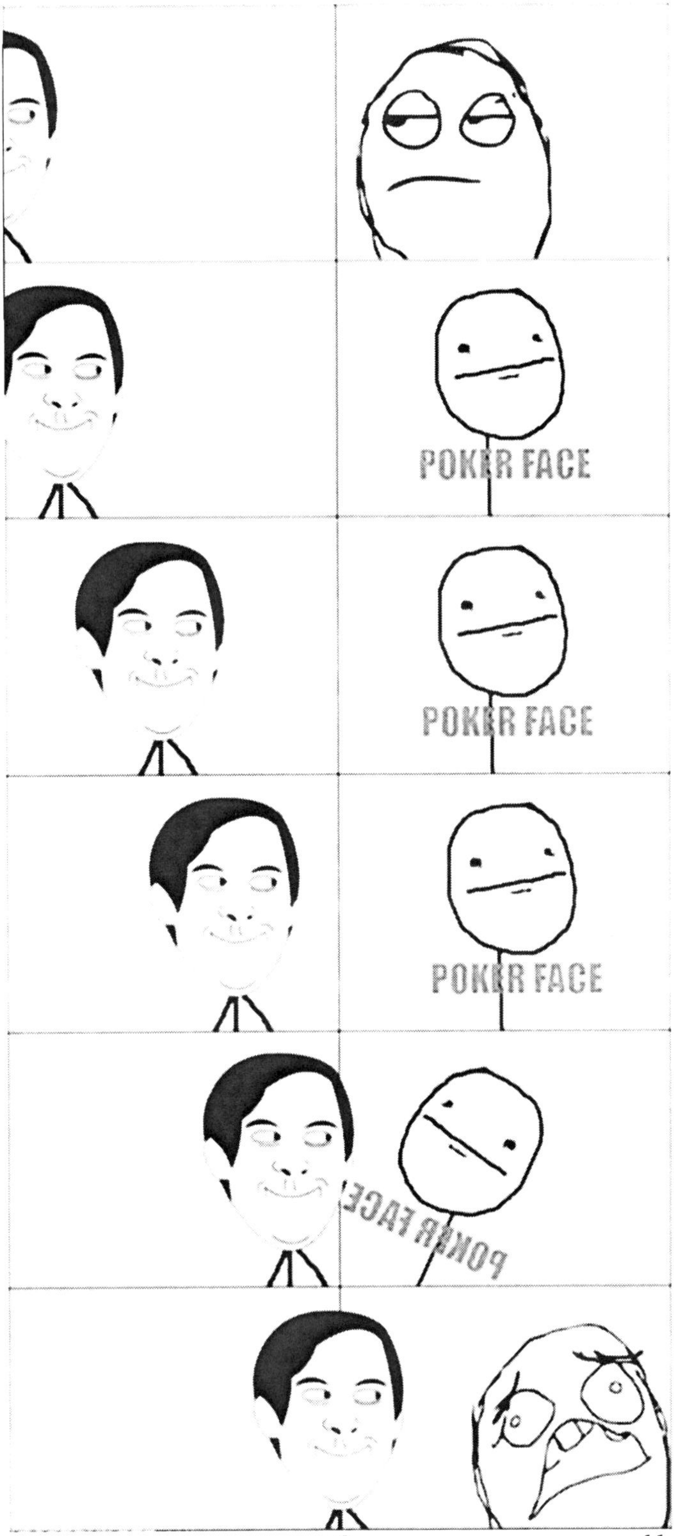
POKER FACE
POKER FACE
POKER FACE

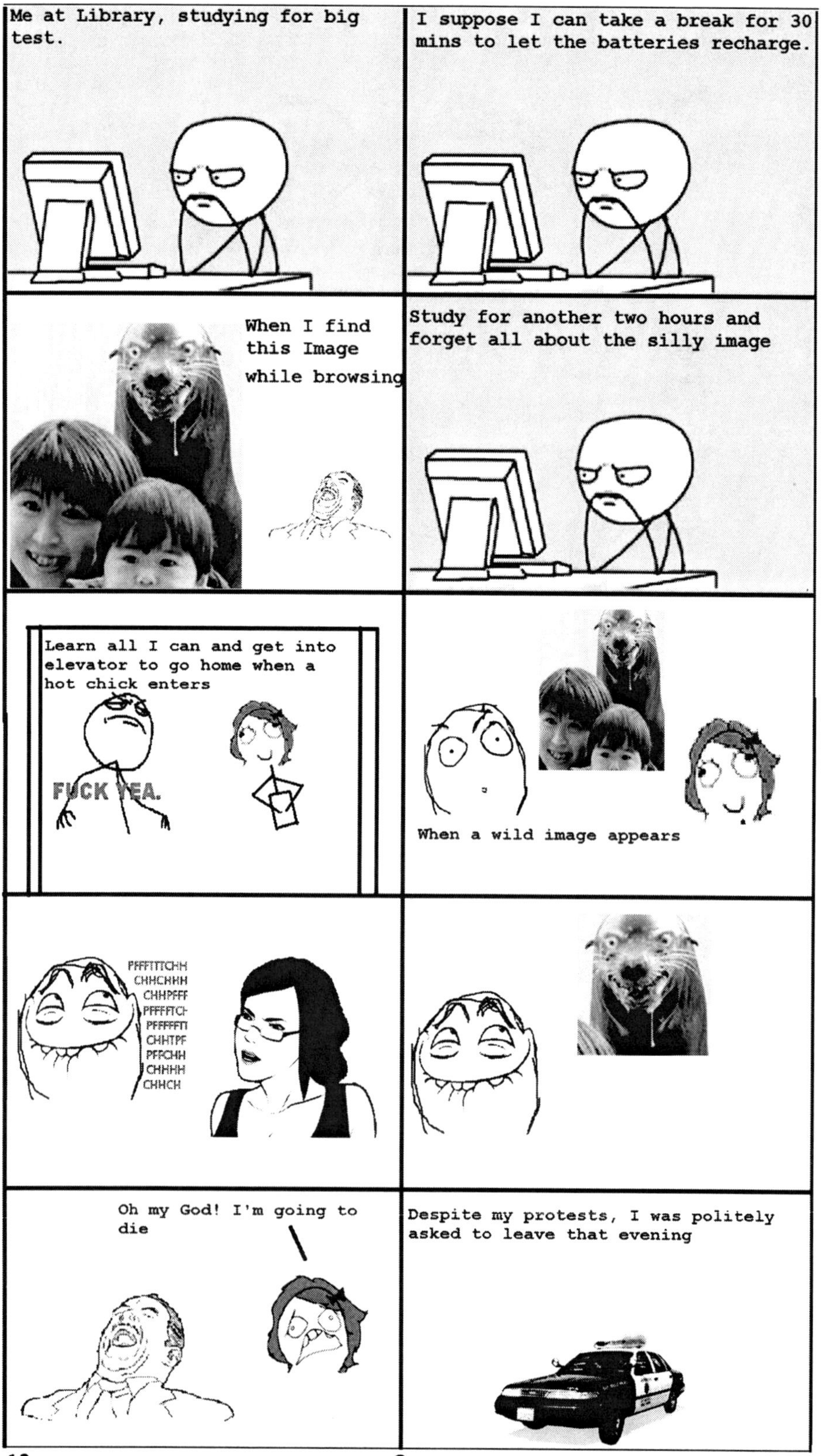
Me at Library, studying for big test.
I suppose I can take a break for 30 mins to let the batteries recharge.
When I find this Image while browsing
Study for another two hours and forget all about the silly image
Learn all I can and get into elevator to go home when a hot chick enters
FUCK YEA.
When a wild image appears
PFFFTTTCHH
CHHCHHH
CHHPFFF
PFFFFTCH
PFFFFFTT
CHHTPF
PFFCHH
CHHHH
CHHCH
Oh my God! I'm going to die
Despite my protests, I was politely asked to leave that evening

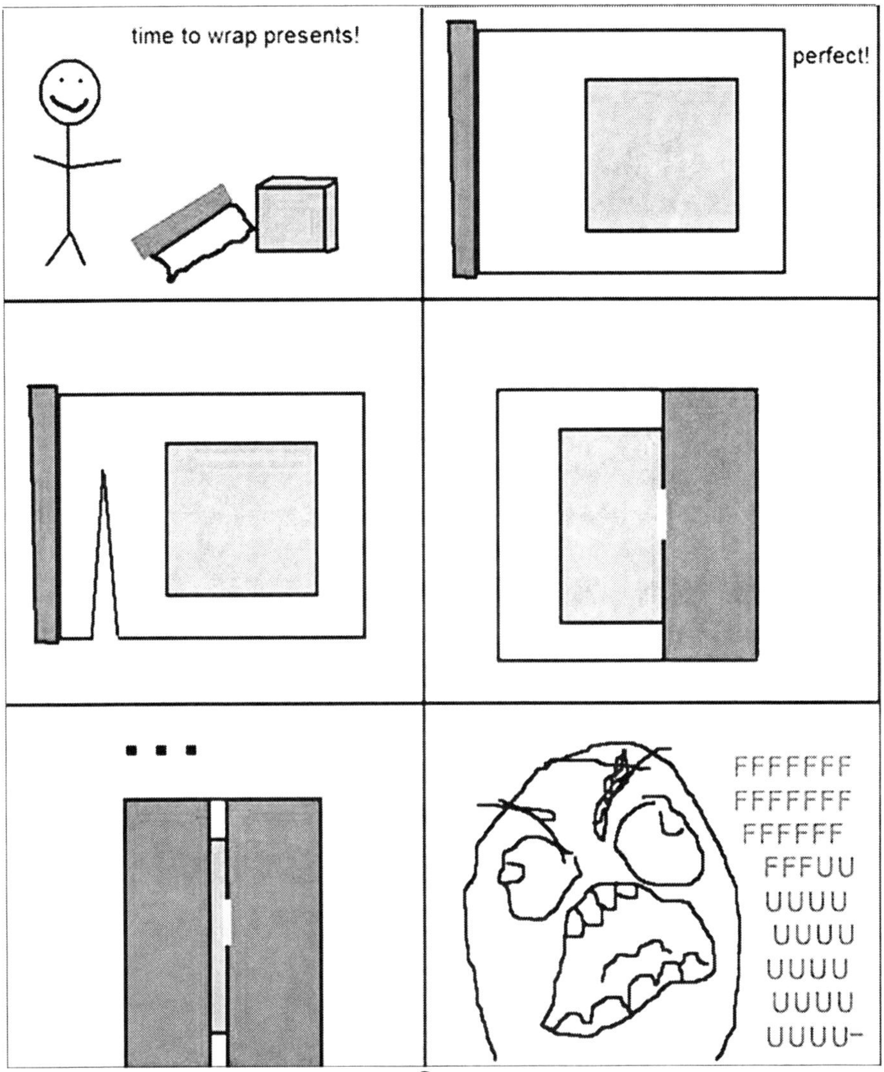
time to wrap presents!
perfect!
...
FFFFFFF
FFFFFFF
FFFFFF
FFFUU
UUUU
UUUU
UUUU
UUUU
UUUU-

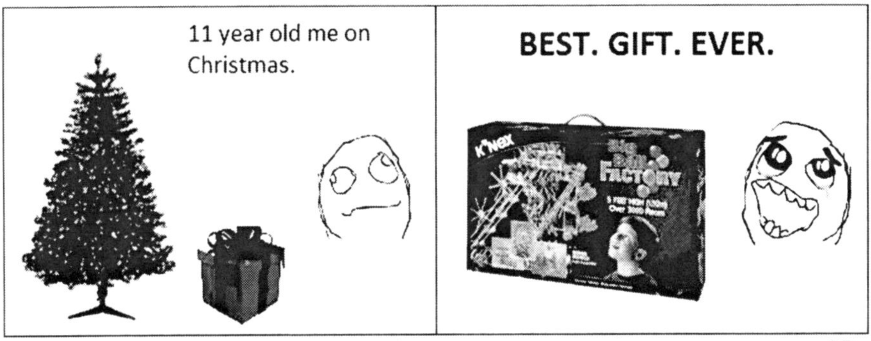
11 year old me on Christmas.
BEST. GIFT. EVER.

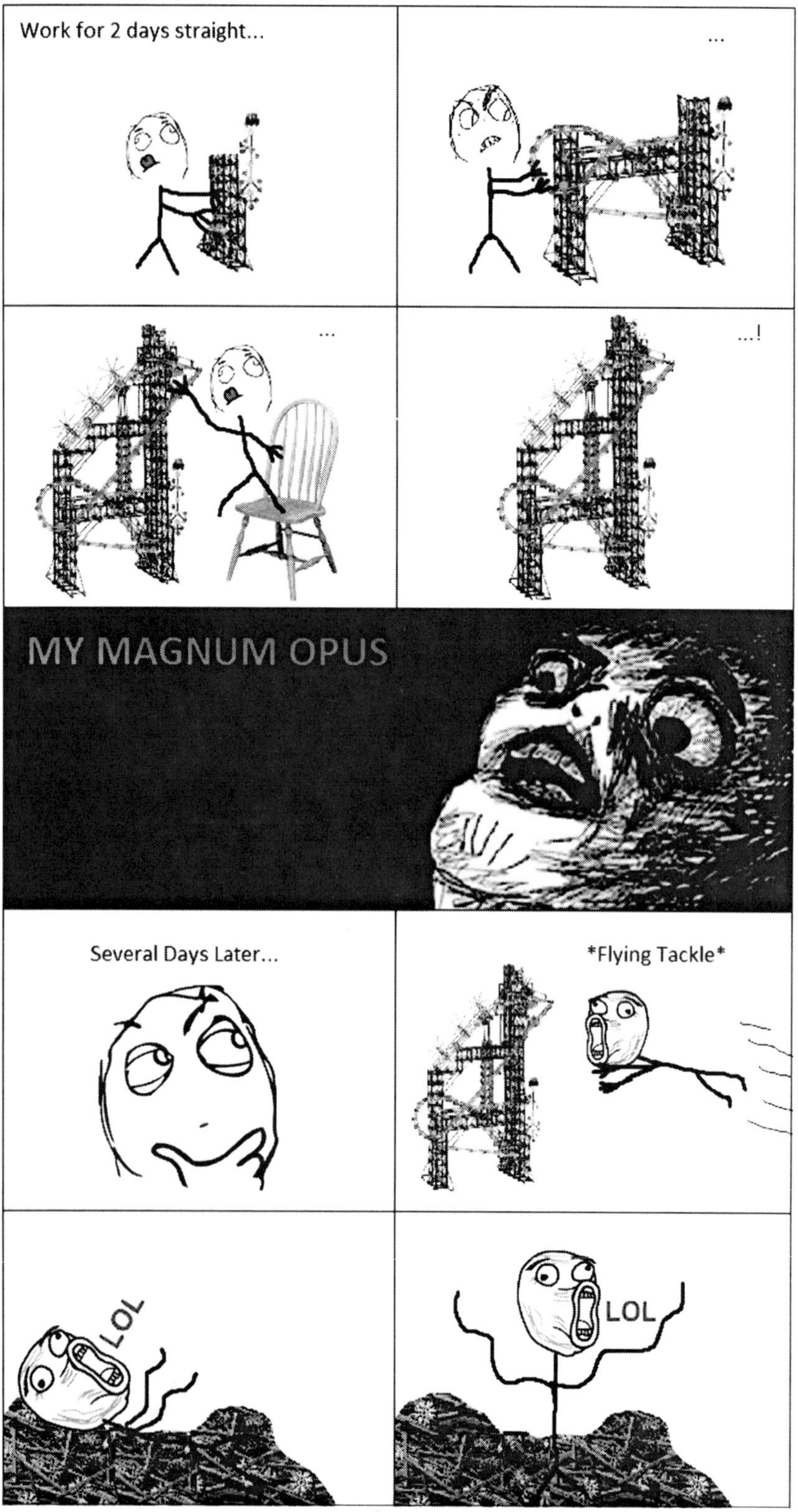
Work for 2 days straight...
...
...
...!
MY MAGNUM OPUS
Several Days Later...
Flying Tackle
LOL
LOL

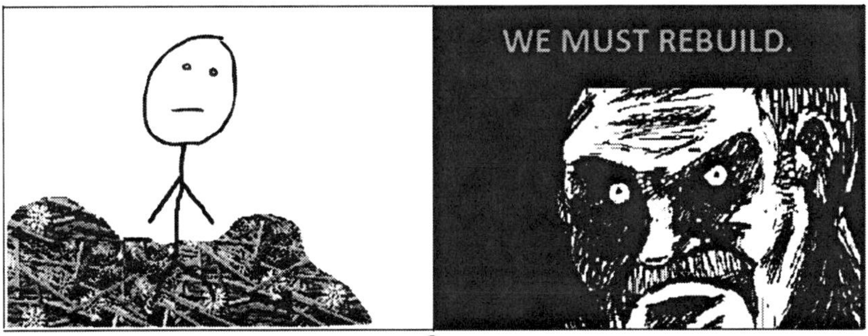
WE MUST REBUILD.

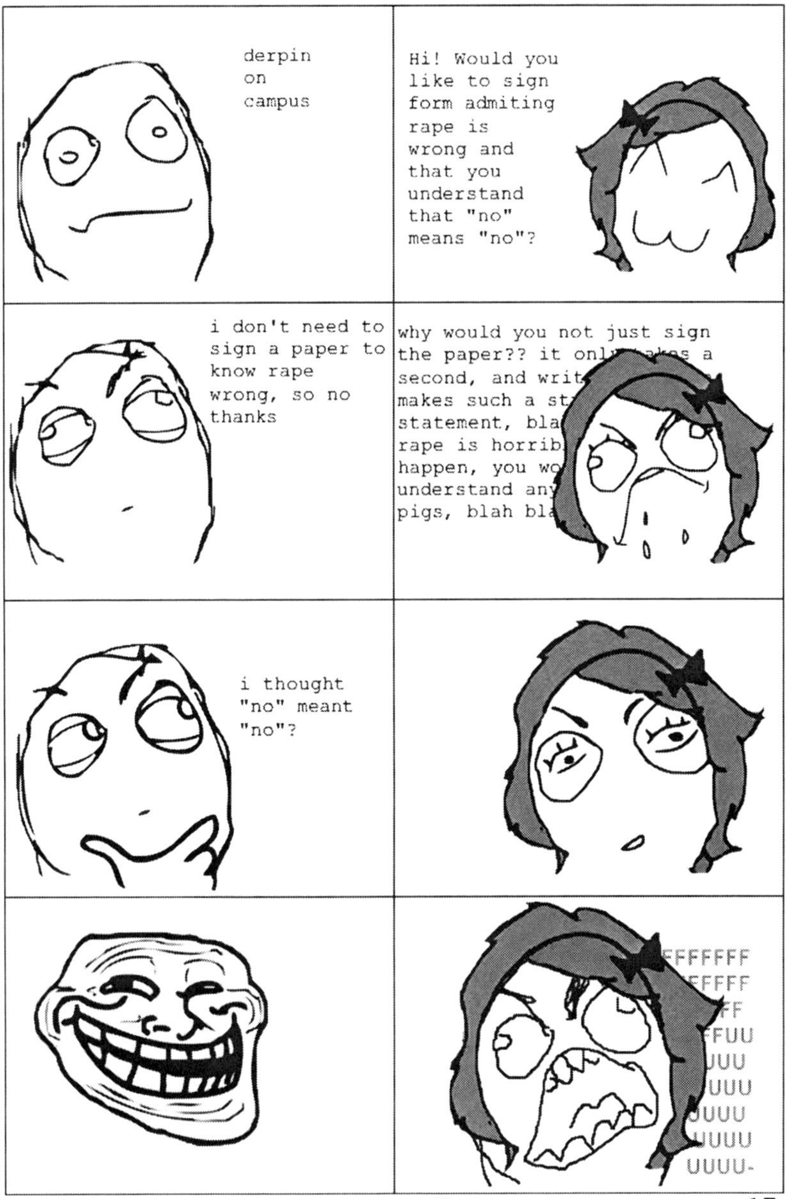
derpin on campus
Hi! Would you like to sign form admiting rape is wrong and that you understand that "no" means "no"?
i don't need to sign a paper to know rape wrong, so no thanks
why would you not just sign the paper?? it onl a second, and writ makes such a st statement, bla rape is horrib happen, you wo understand any pigs, blah bla
i thought "no" meant "no"?
FFFFFFF FFFFF FF FFUU UUU UUU UUU UUUU UUUU-

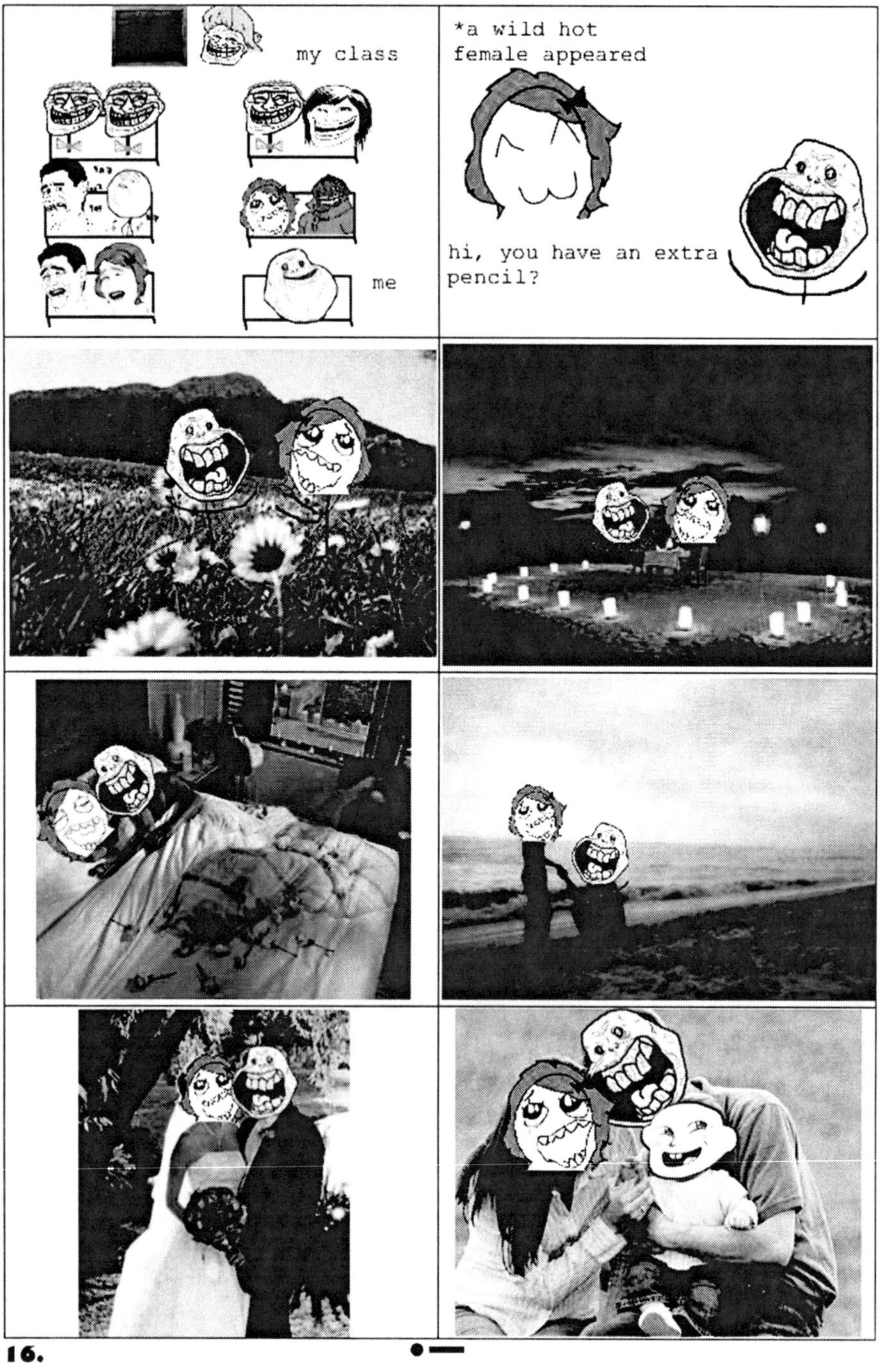
my class
me
*a wild hot
female appeared
hi, you have an extra
pencil?

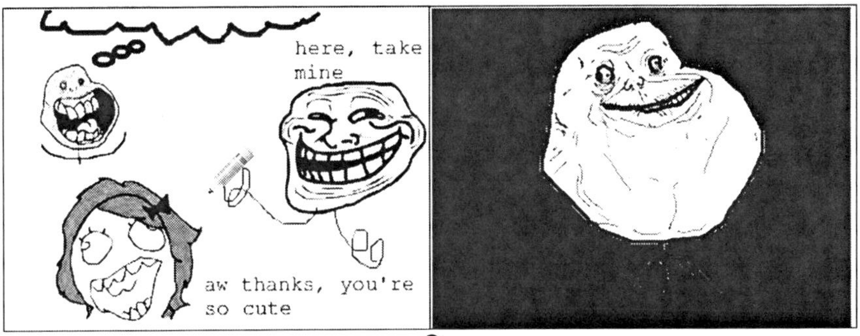
here, take mine
aw thanks, you're so cute

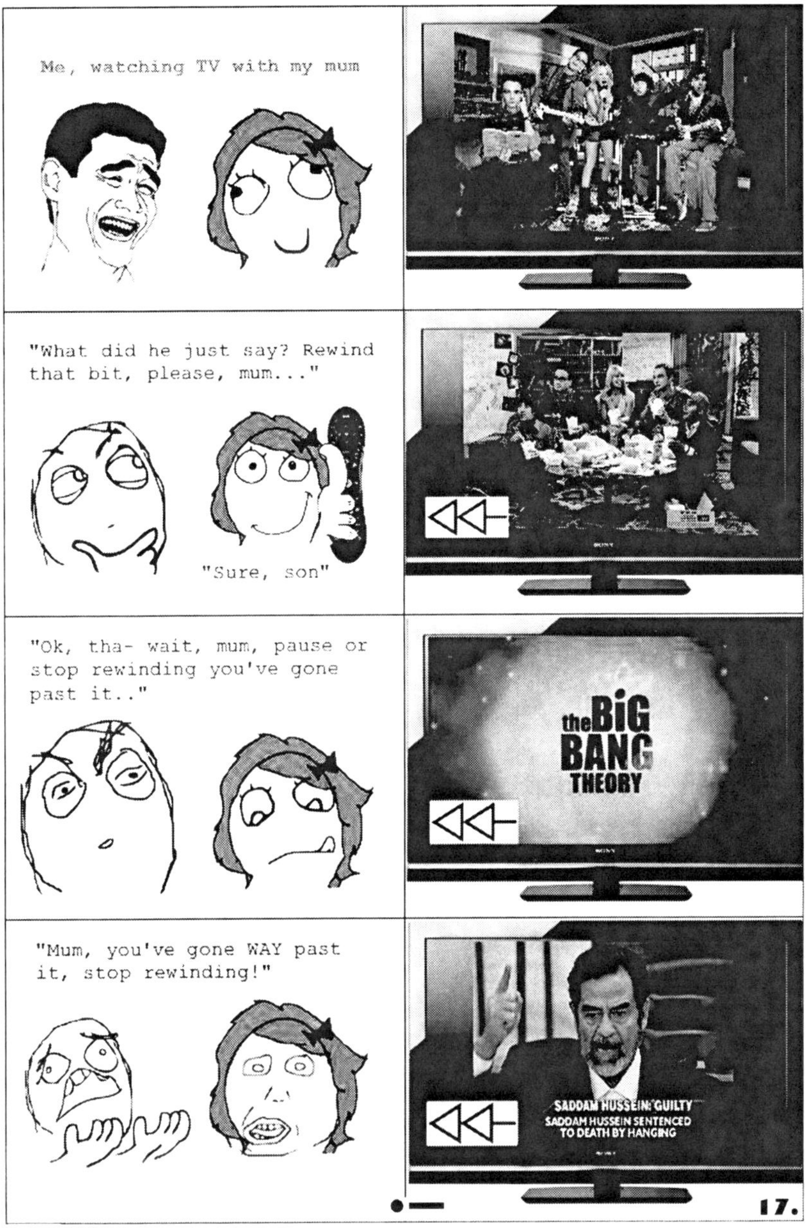
Me, watching TV with my mum
"What did he just say? Rewind that bit, please, mum..."
"Sure, son"
"Ok, tha- wait, mum, pause or stop rewinding you've gone past it.."
theBIG BANG THEORY
"Mum, you've gone WAY past it, stop rewinding!"
SADDAM HUSSEIN: GUILTY
SADDAM HUSSEIN SENTENCED TO DEATH BY HANGING

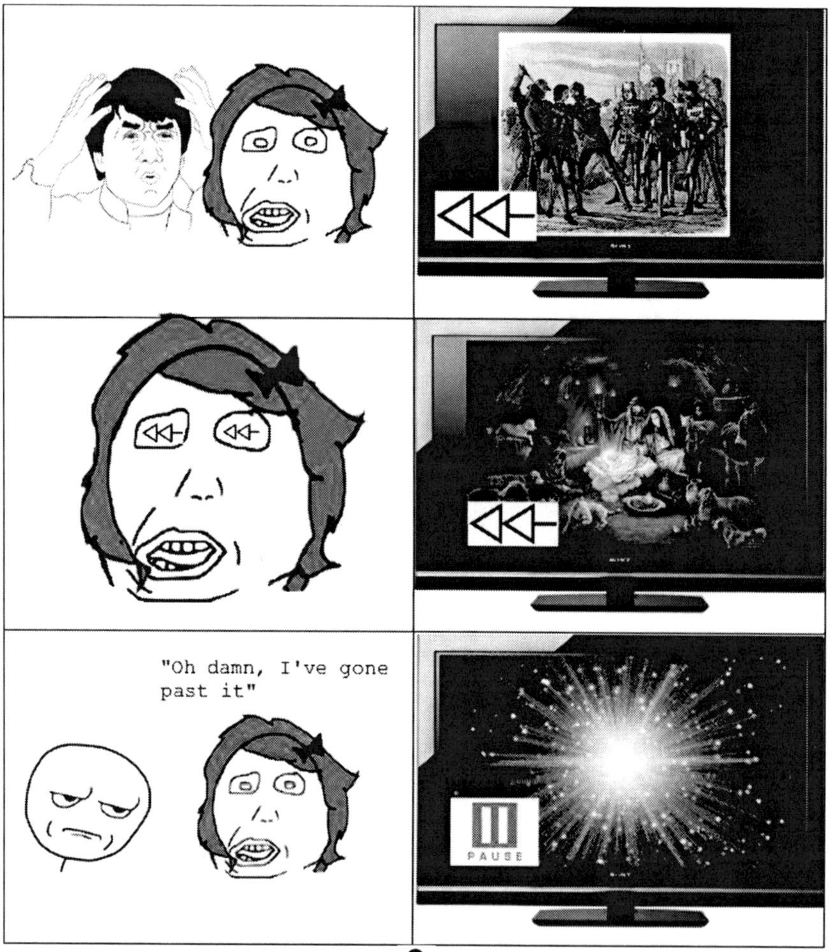
"Oh damn, I've gone past it"
PAUSE

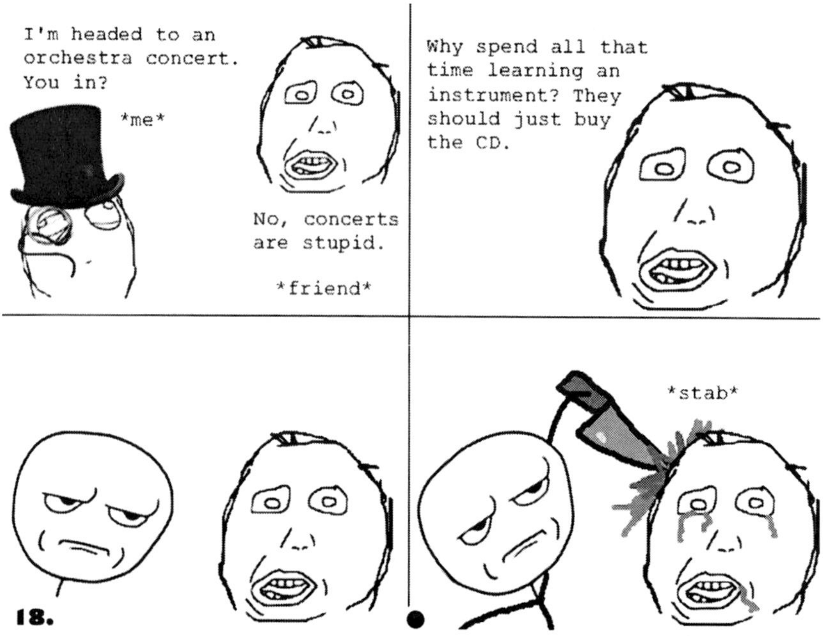
I'm headed to an orchestra concert. You in?
me
No, concerts are stupid.
friend
Why spend all that time learning an instrument? They should just buy the CD.
stab

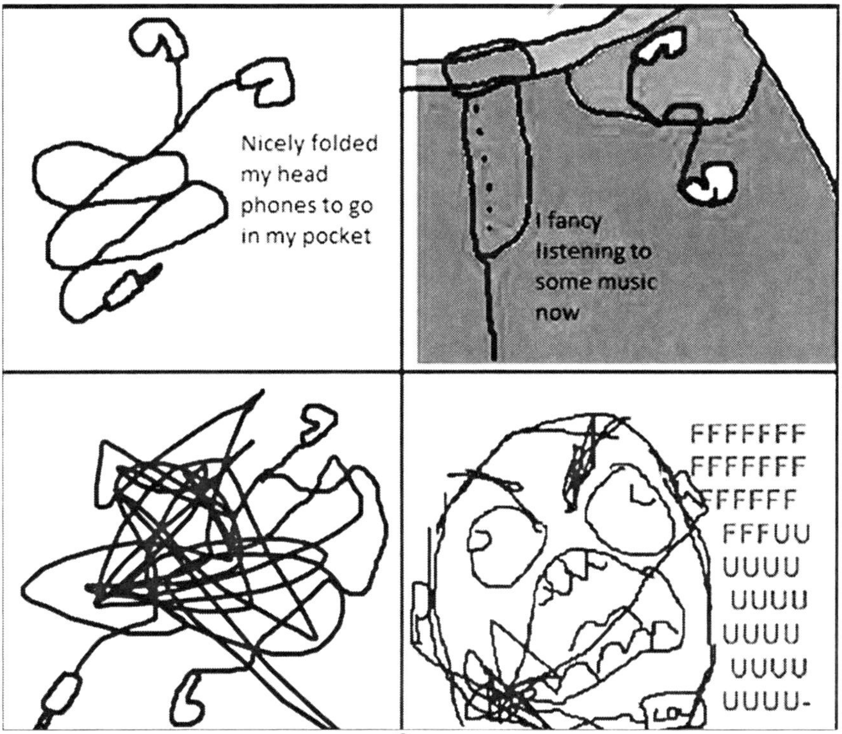
Nicely folded my head phones to go in my pocket
I fancy listening to some music now
FFFFFFF
FFFFFFF
FFFFFF
FFFUU
UUUU
UUUU
UUUU
UUUU
UUUU-

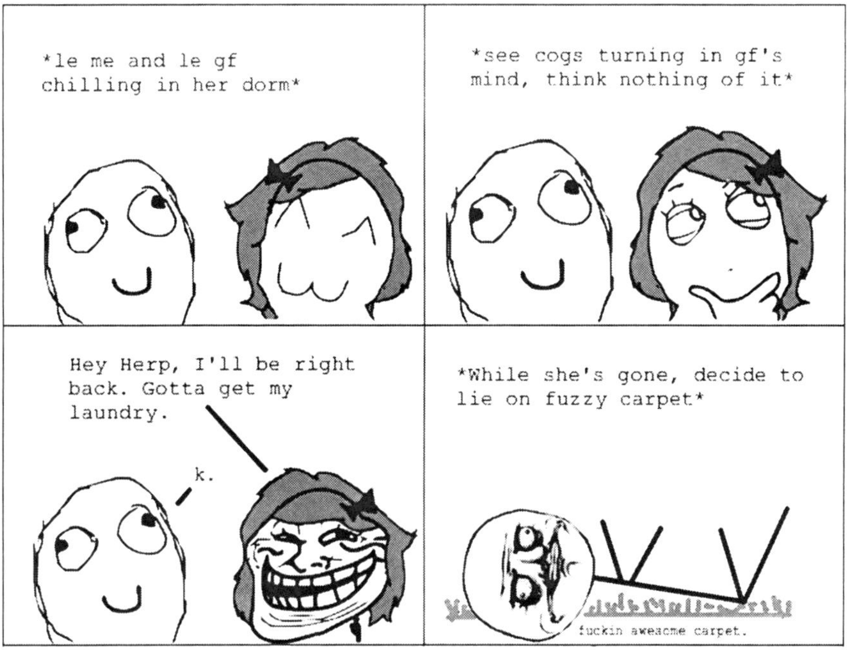
le me and le gf chilling in her dorm
see cogs turning in gf's mind, think nothing of it
Hey Herp, I'll be right back. Gotta get my laundry.
k.
While she's gone, decide to lie on fuzzy carpet
fuckin aweacme carpet.

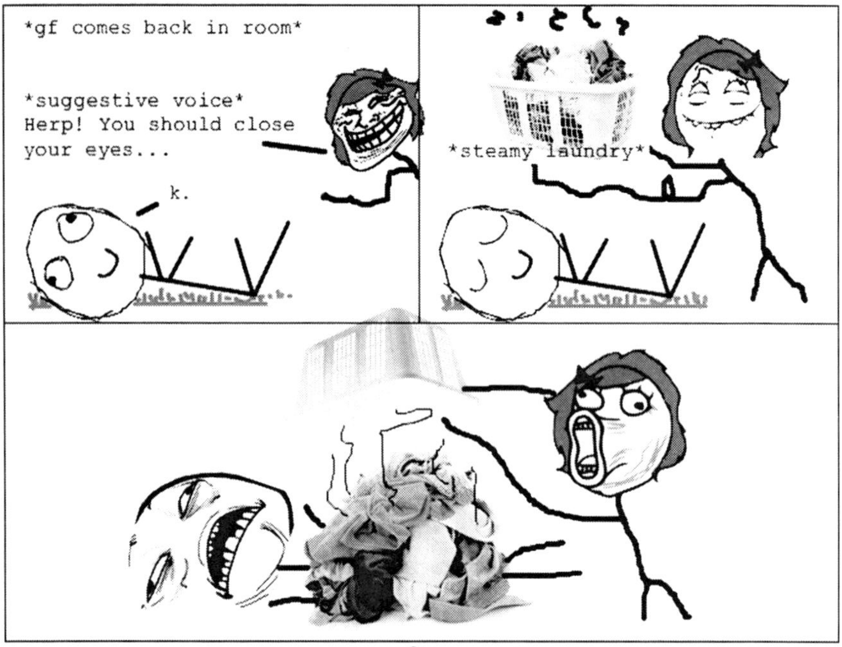
gf comes back in room
suggestive voice
Herp! You should close your eyes...
k.
steamy laundry

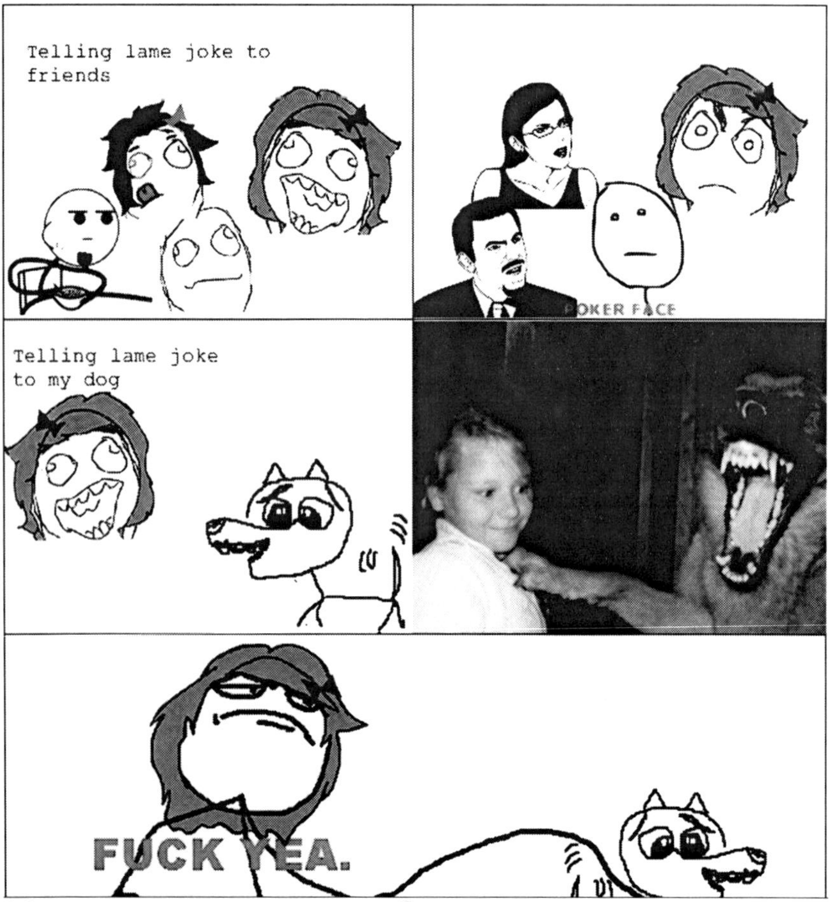
Telling lame joke to friends
POKER FACE
Telling lame joke to my dog
FUCK YEA.

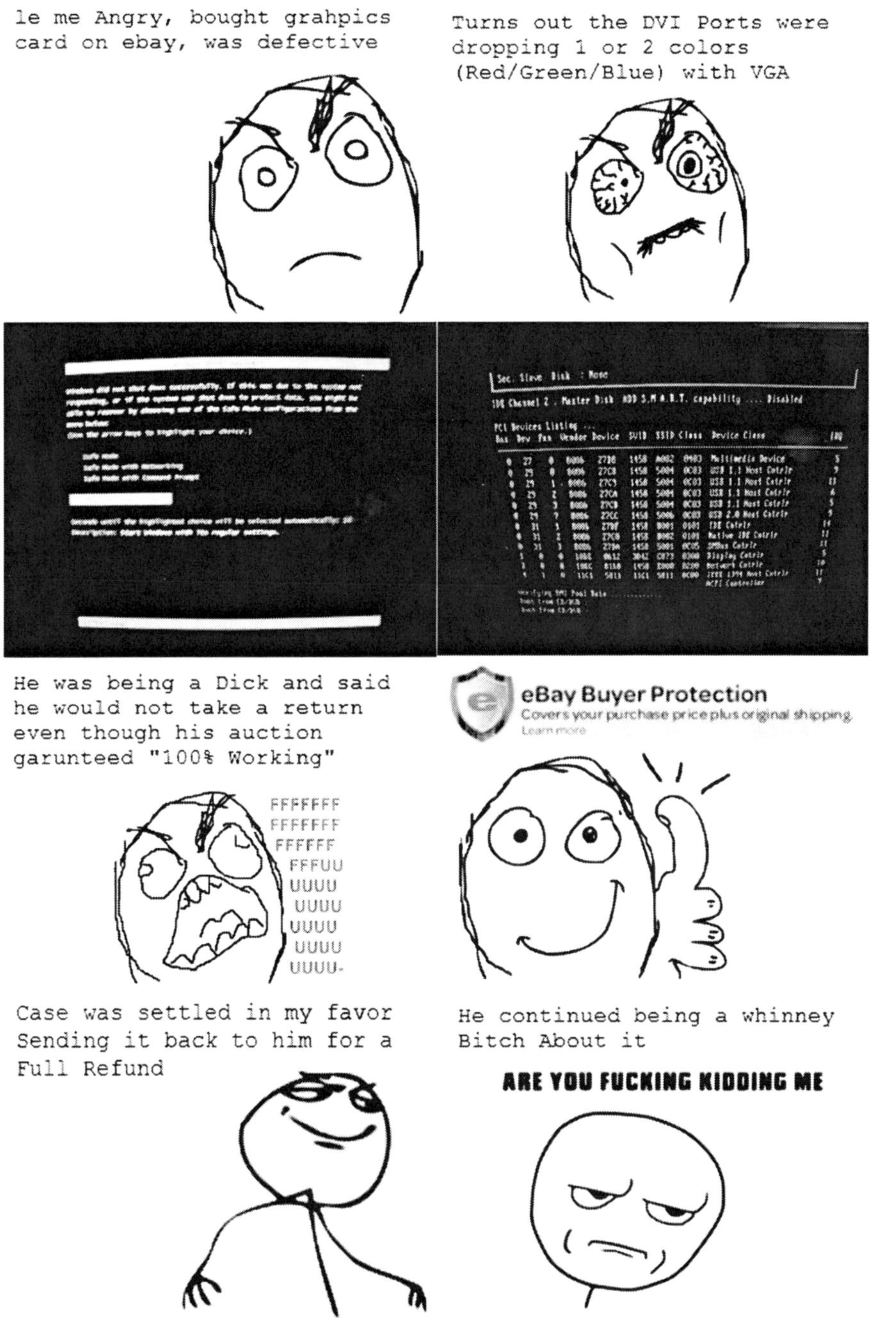

le me Angry, bought grahpics card on ebay, was defective
Turns out the DVI Ports were dropping 1 or 2 colors (Red/Green/Blue) with VGA
He was being a Dick and said he would not take a return even though his auction garunteed "100% Working"
eBay Buyer Protection
Covers your purchase price plus original shipping
FFFFFFF
FFFFFFF
FFFFFF
FFFUU
UUUU
UUUU
UUUU
UUUU
UUUU
Case was settled in my favor Sending it back to him for a Full Refund
He continued being a whinney Bitch About it
ARE YOU FUCKING KIDDING ME

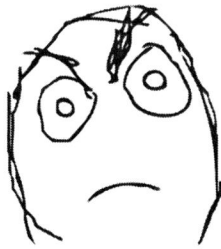

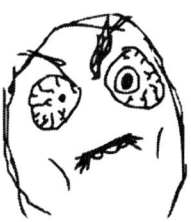

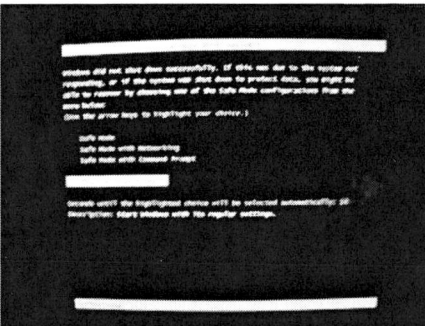

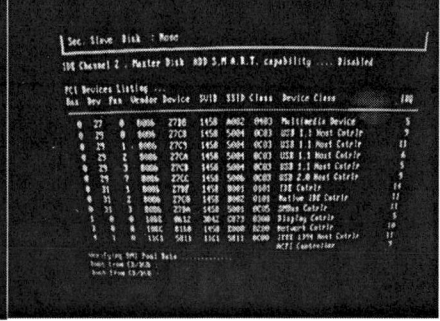

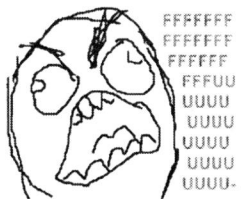

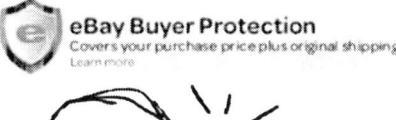

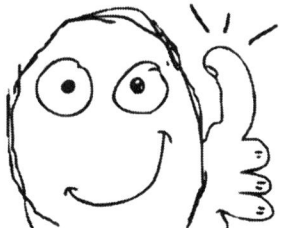

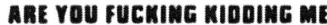

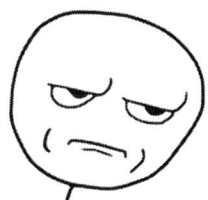

A Wild Idea Appeared!

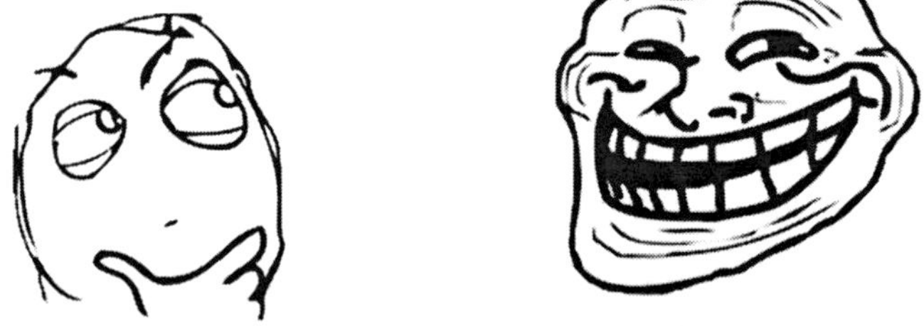

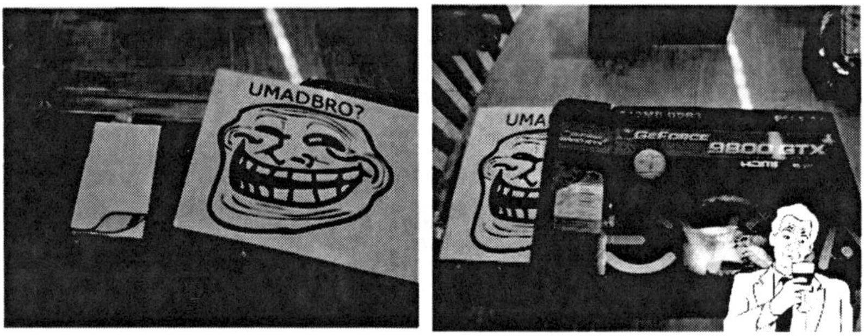
UMADBRO?
9800 GTX

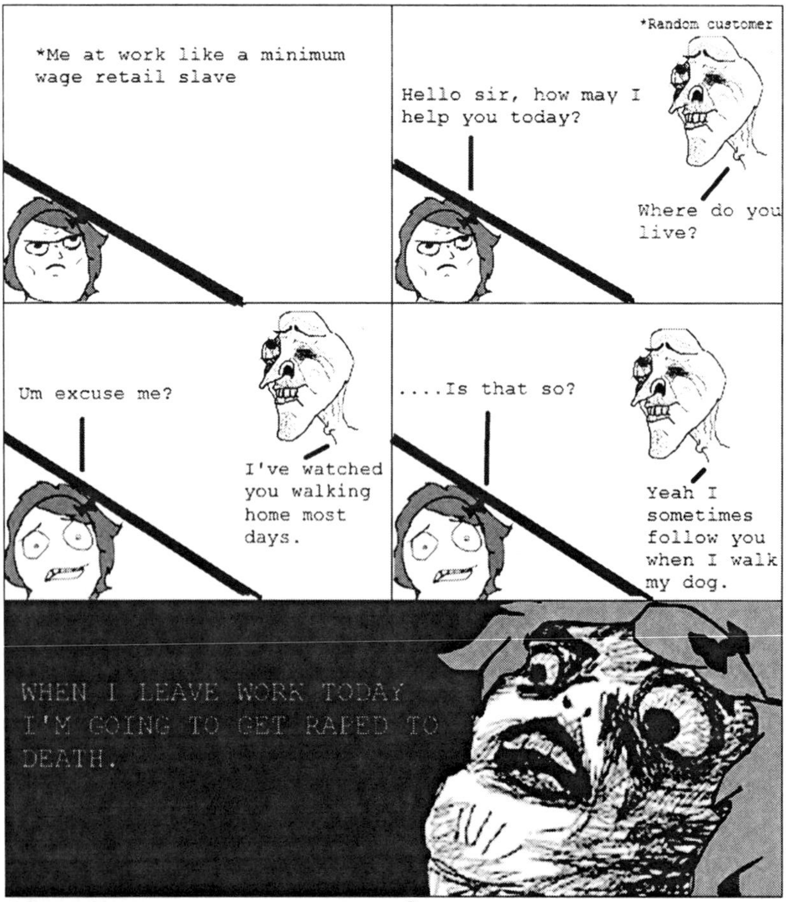
*Me at work like a minimum wage retail slave
*Random customer
Hello sir, how may I help you today?
Where do you live?
Um excuse me?
I've watched you walking home most days.
....Is that so?
Yeah I sometimes follow you when I walk my dog.
WHEN I LEAVE WORK TODAY I'M GOING TO GET RAPED TO DEATH.

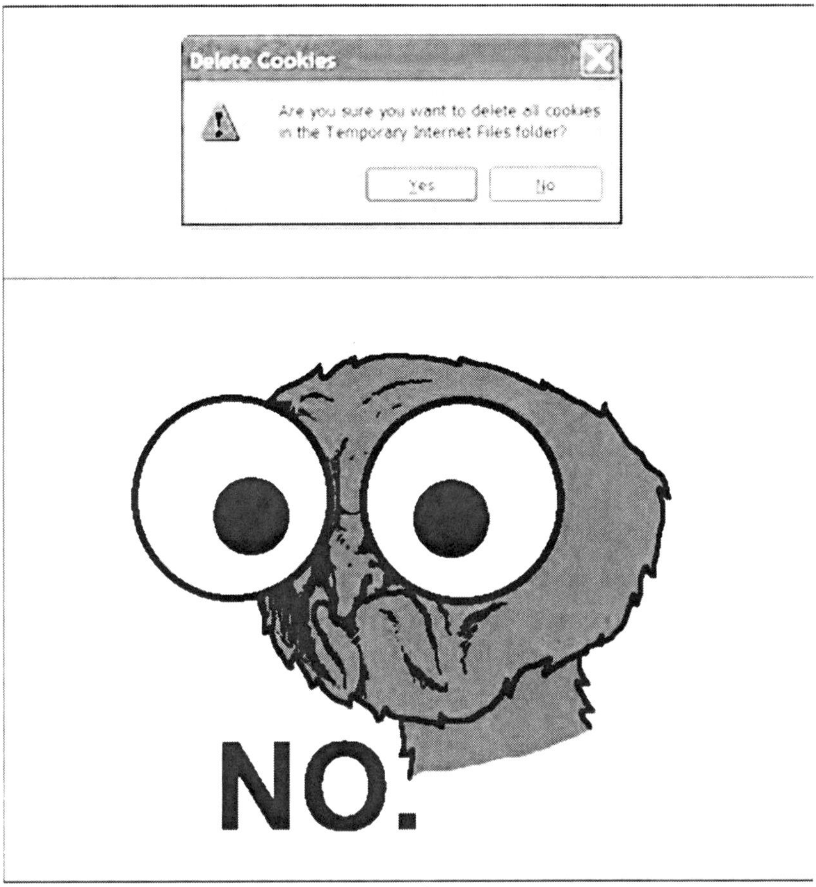
Delete Cookies
Are you sure you want to delete all cookies in the Temporary Internet Files folder?
Yes
No
NO.

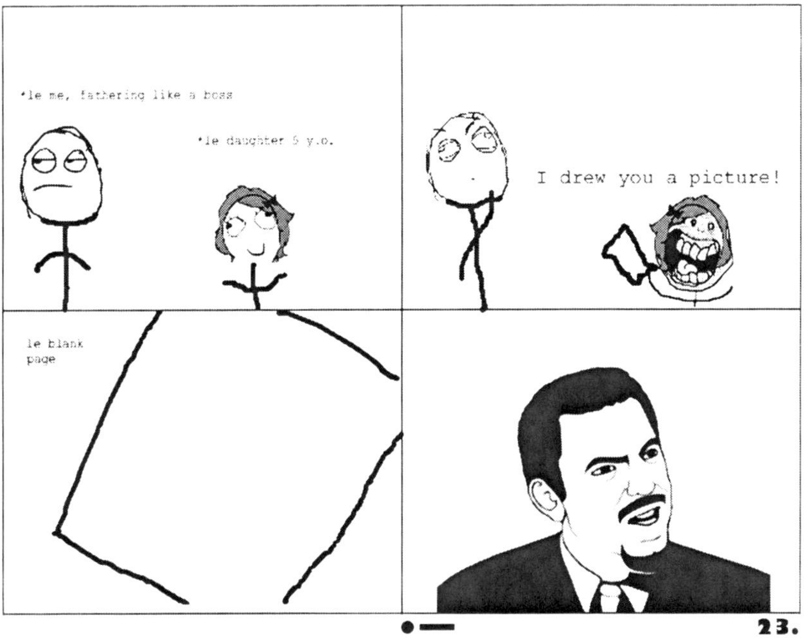
*le me, fathering like a boss
*le daughter 5 y.o.
I drew you a picture!
le blank page

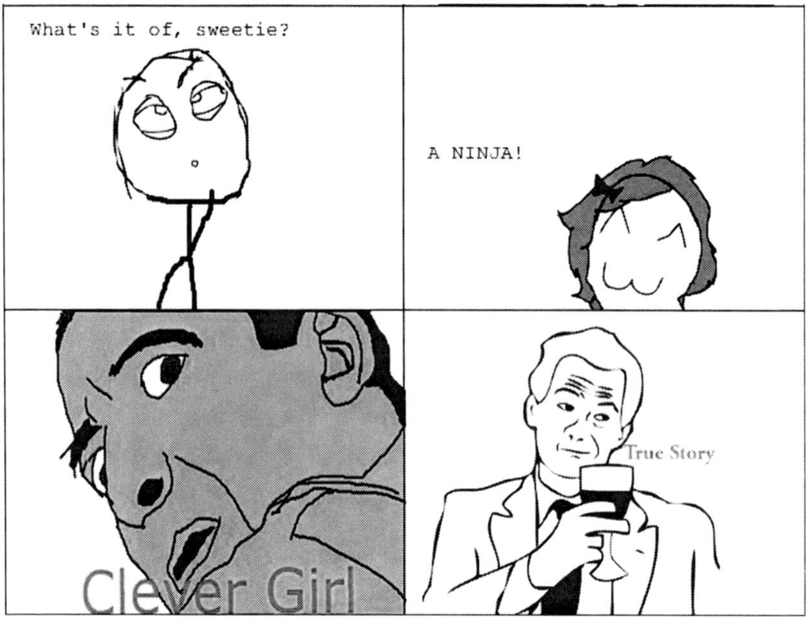
What's it of, sweetie?
A NINJA!
Clever Girl
True Story

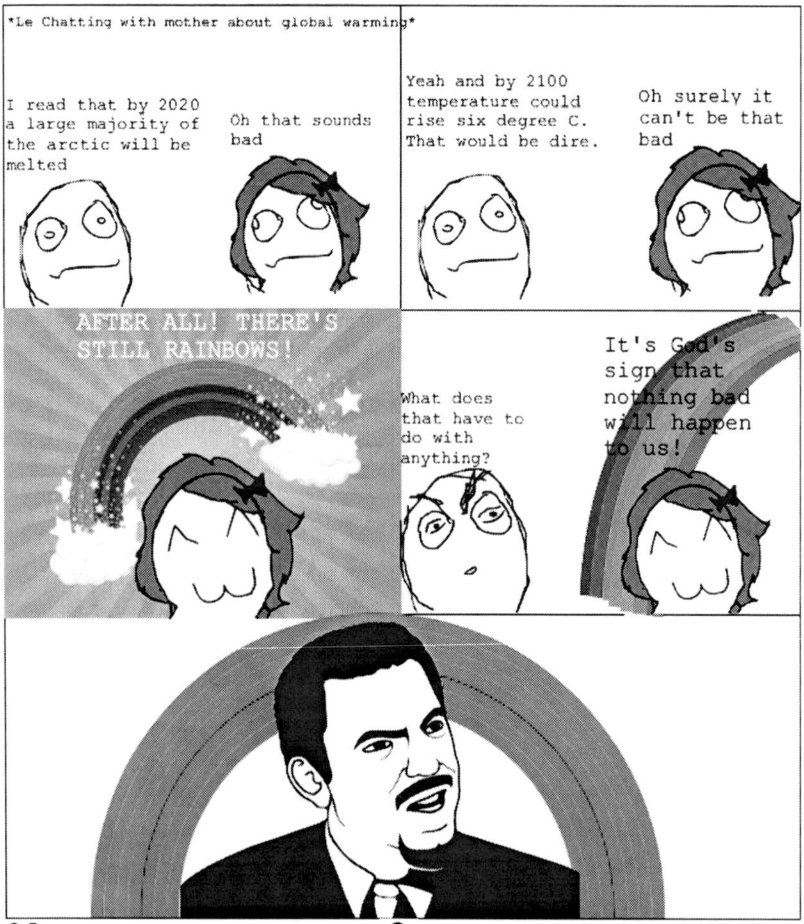
Le Chatting with mother about global warming
I read that by 2020 a large majority of the arctic will be melted
Oh that sounds bad
Yeah and by 2100 temperature could rise six degree C. That would be dire.
Oh surely it can't be that bad
AFTER ALL! THERE'S STILL RAINBOWS!
What does that have to do with anything?
It's God's sign that nothing bad will happen to us!

Pfft... Some lame 80's movie.

Never heard of it, eh?

The 50'S?????
I thought this movie would be in the future!!

Fucking 2 hours of this bullshit.

Ohhhhh....

LOL

GEORGE

Y u no go to dance?

 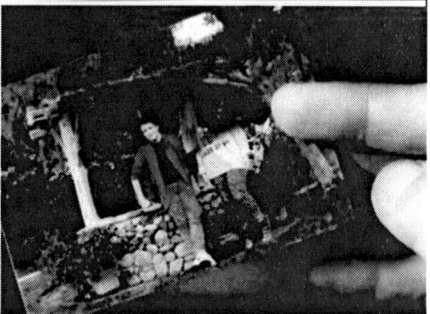

GAAHHHHHHH

 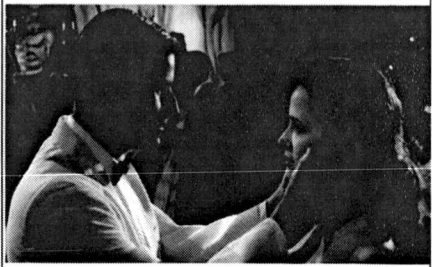

26.

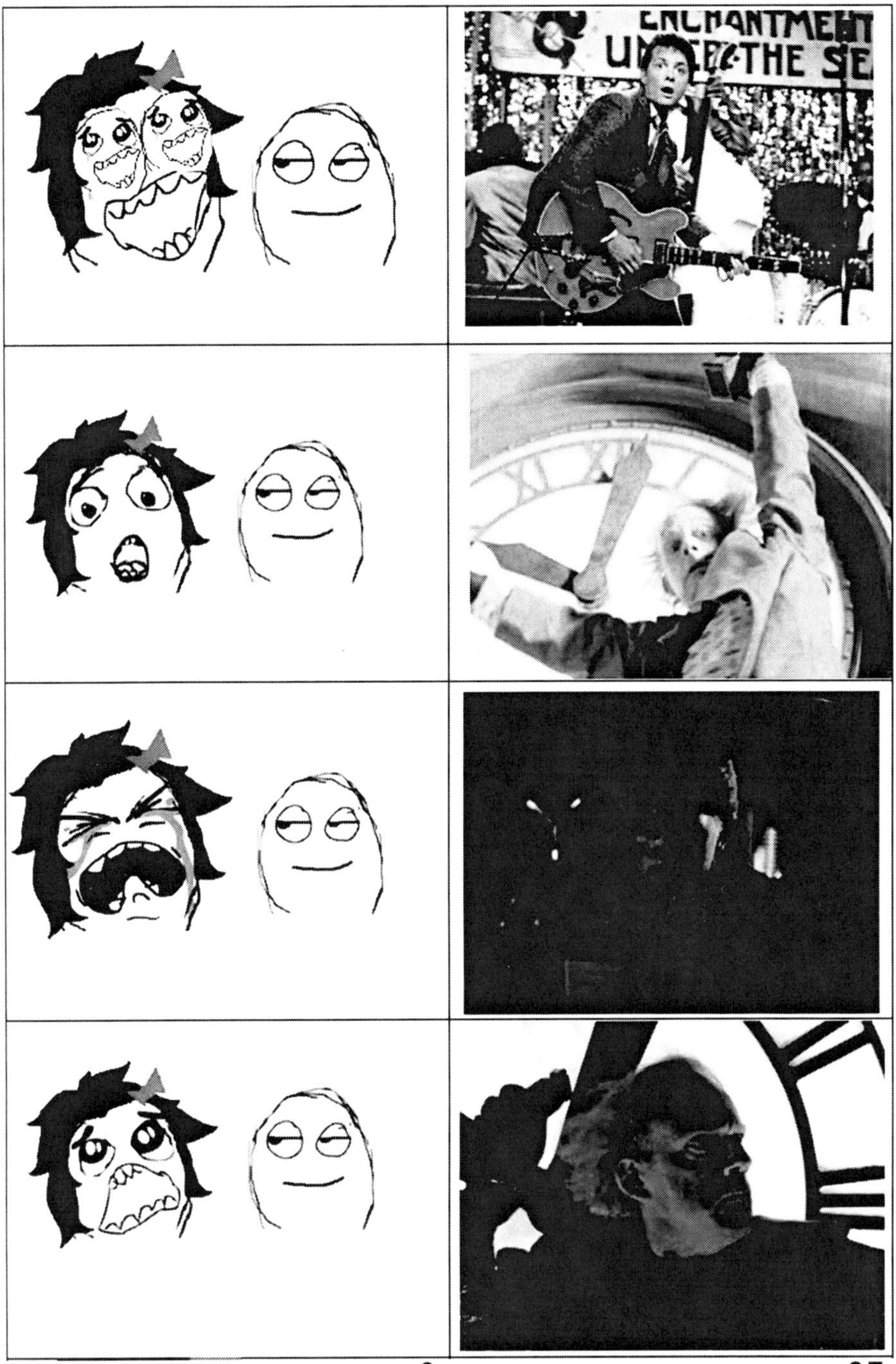

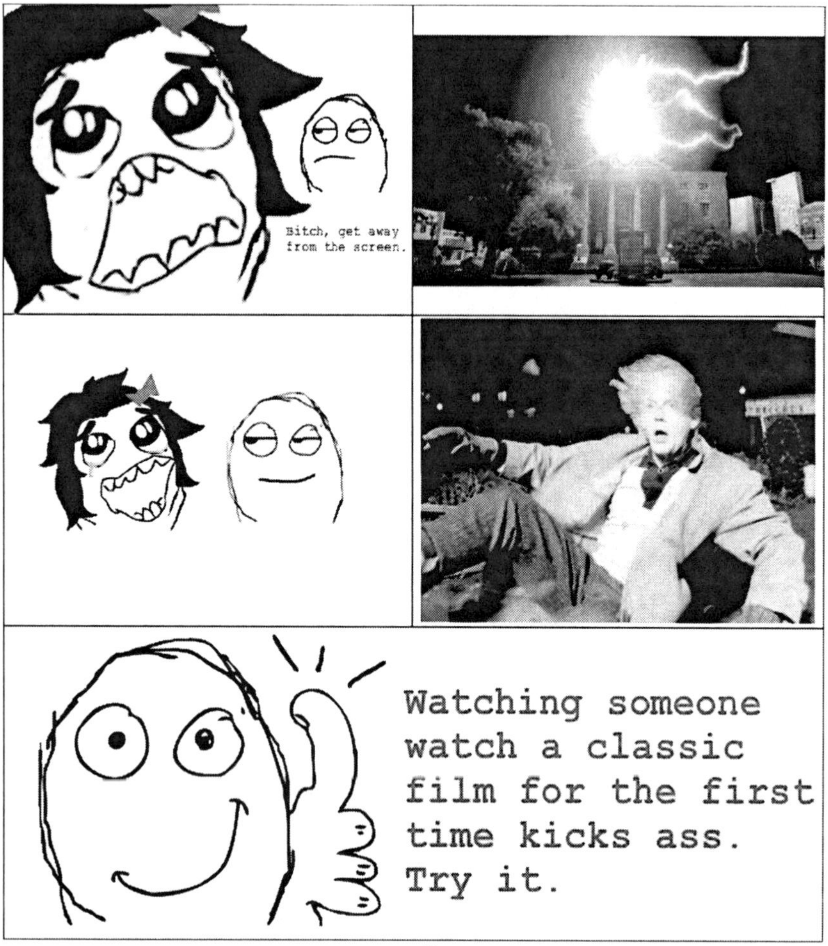
Bitch, get away
from the screen.
Watching someone
watch a classic
film for the first
time kicks ass.
Try it.

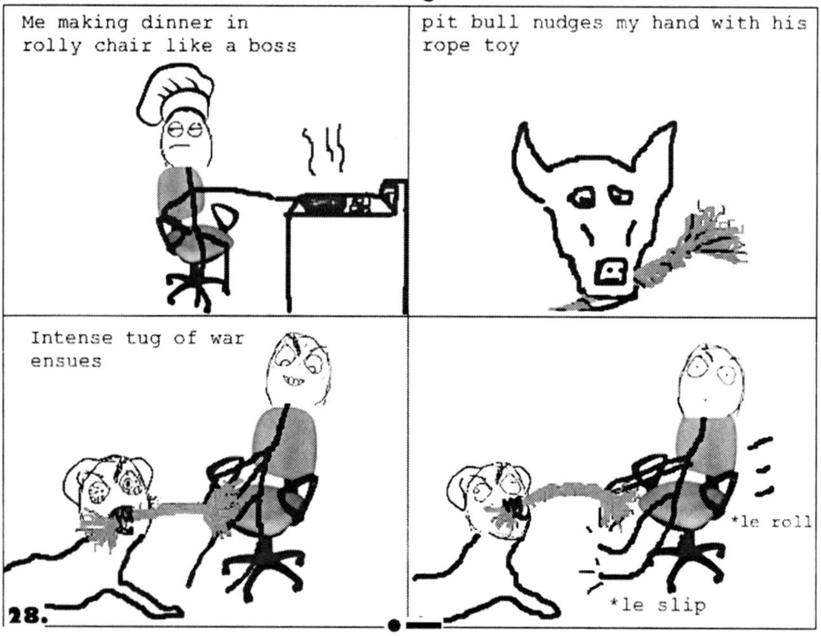
Me making dinner in
rolly chair like a boss
pit bull nudges my hand with his
rope toy
Intense tug of war
ensues
*le roll
*le slip

Let's watch The Princess Bride!

Ok, I guess we can watch your stupid princess movie I've never seen.

Don't worry, the title is supposed to sound lame. You're just like Fred Savage and he loved it by the end.

obvious bad start

Who's Fred Savage?

But listen to all the witty banter! You love witty banter!

This is dumb and old looking.

You can totally tell that's a costume!

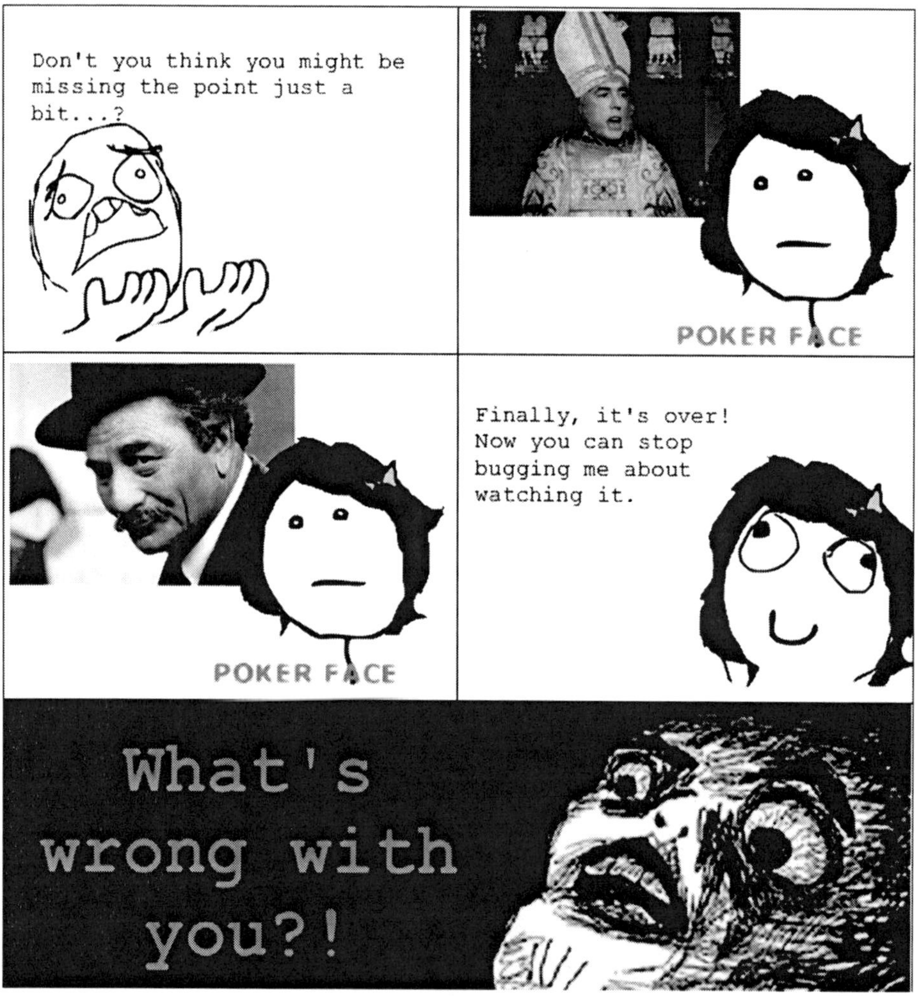
Don't you think you might be missing the point just a bit...?
POKER FACE
POKER FACE
Finally, it's over! Now you can stop bugging me about watching it.
What's wrong with you?!

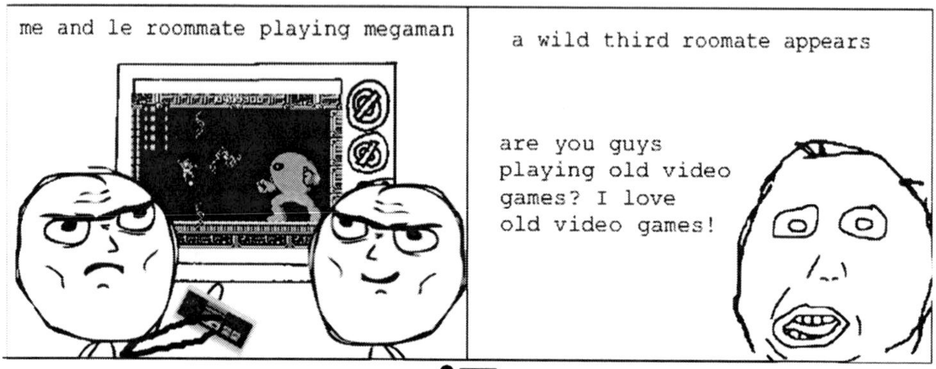
me and le roommate playing megaman
a wild third roomate appears
are you guys playing old video games? I love old video games!

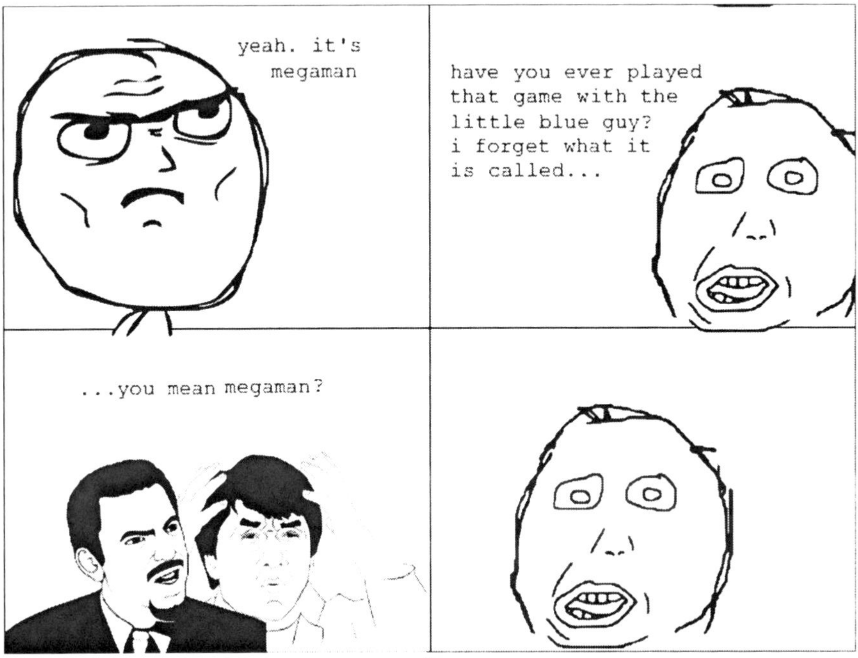
yeah. it's megaman
have you ever played that game with the little blue guy? i forget what it is called...
...you mean megaman?

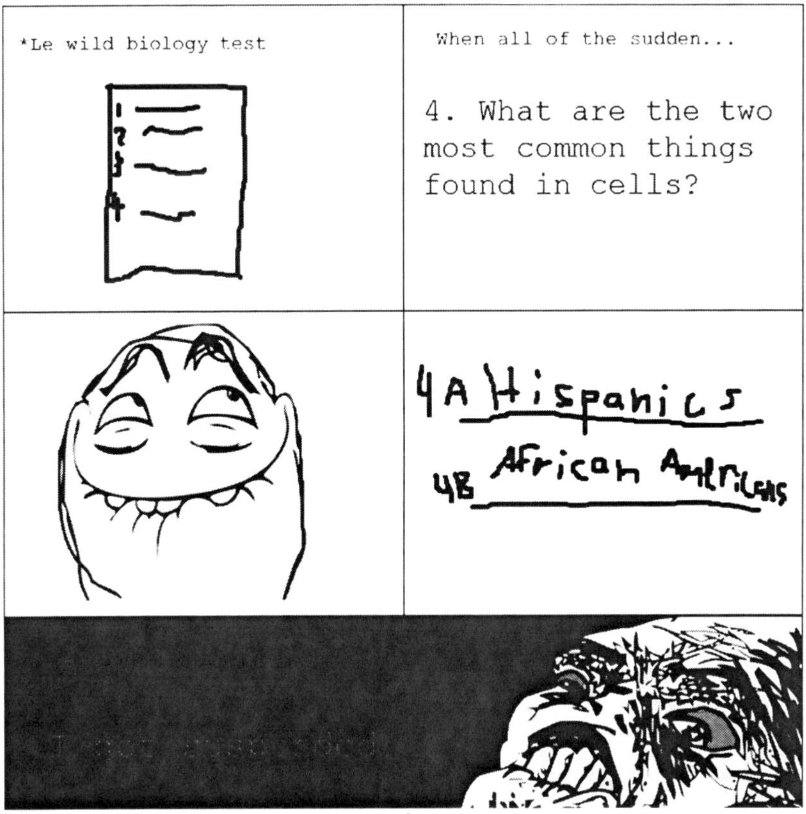
*Le wild biology test
When all of the sudden...
4. What are the two most common things found in cells?
4A Hispanics
4B African Americans

making le kraft dinner
Kraft Dinner
stir the pot...
Okay. Time to take a noodle out to test if the noodles are cooked enough.
you are...
THE CHOSEN ONE

I want you to derp my derpina hehe!!!
le sexytime text with the girlfriend
Derp is that your new phone? It looks so cool! And I really wanna see it? Can I pretty please!?!
le sister
hand le phone
Yeah it is pretty Cool check it out!!
Derpina texted you she says...
I want you to derp my... OMG WHAT?!
POKER FACE

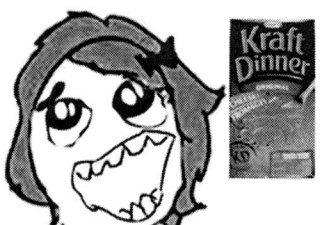

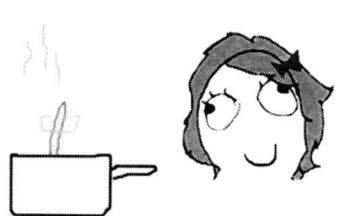

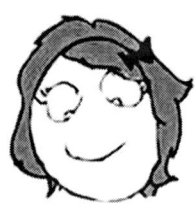

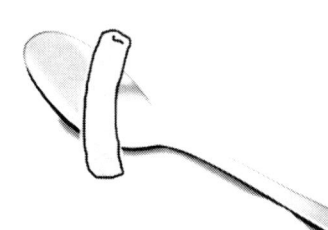

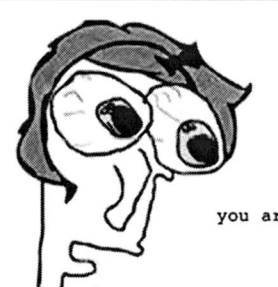

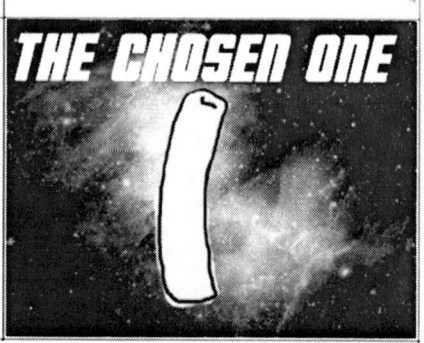

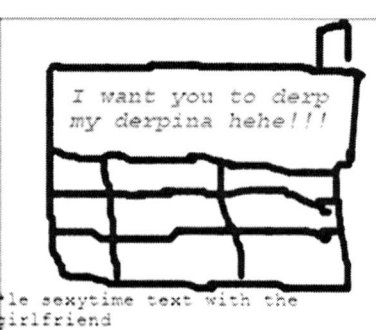

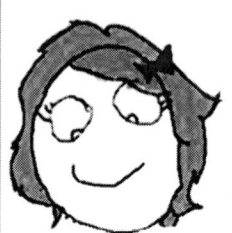

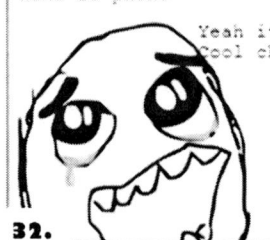

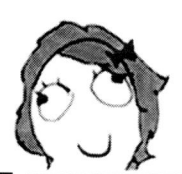

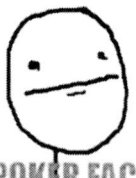

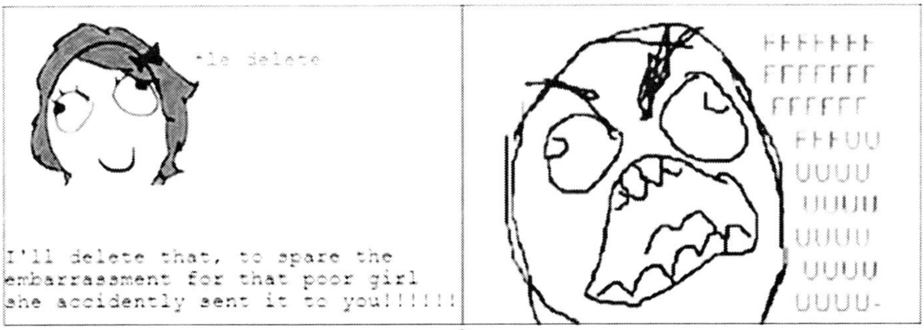
*le delete
I'll delete that, to spare the embarrassment for that poor girl she accidently sent it to you!!!!!!
FFFFFFF
FFFFFFF
FFFFFF
FFFUU
UUUU
UUUU
UUUU
UUUU
UUUU-

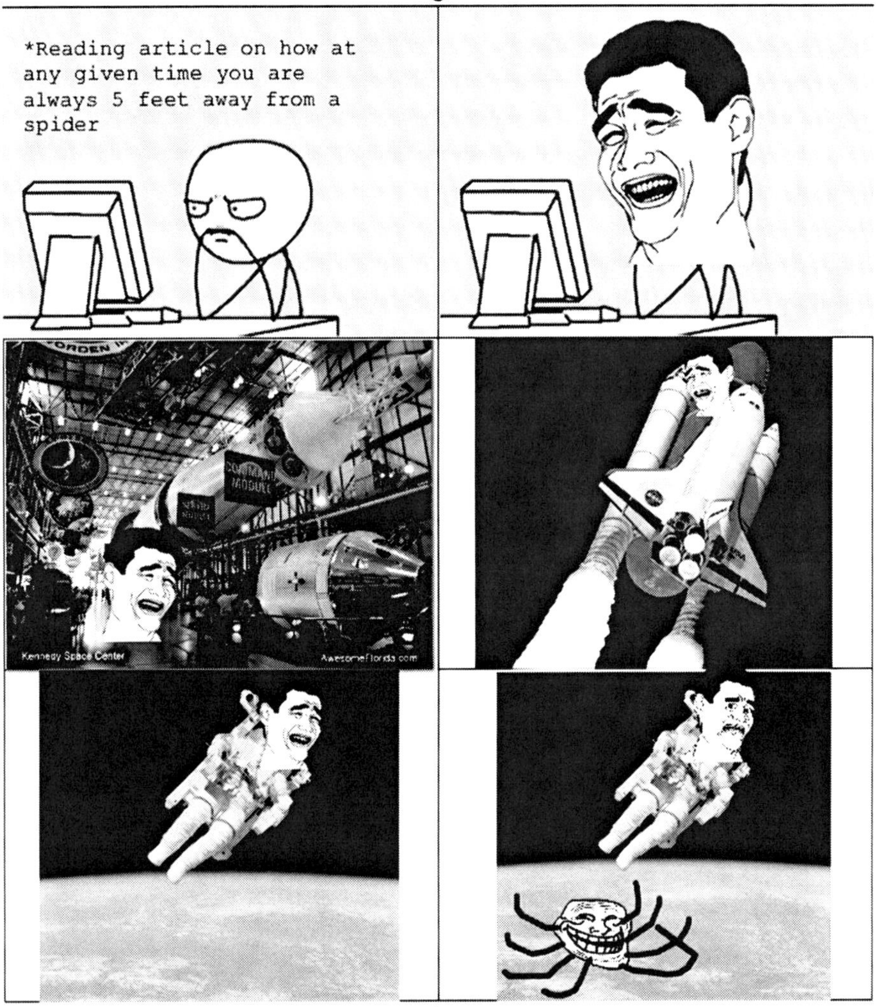
*Reading article on how at any given time you are always 5 feet away from a spider
Kennedy Space Center
AwesomeFlorida.com

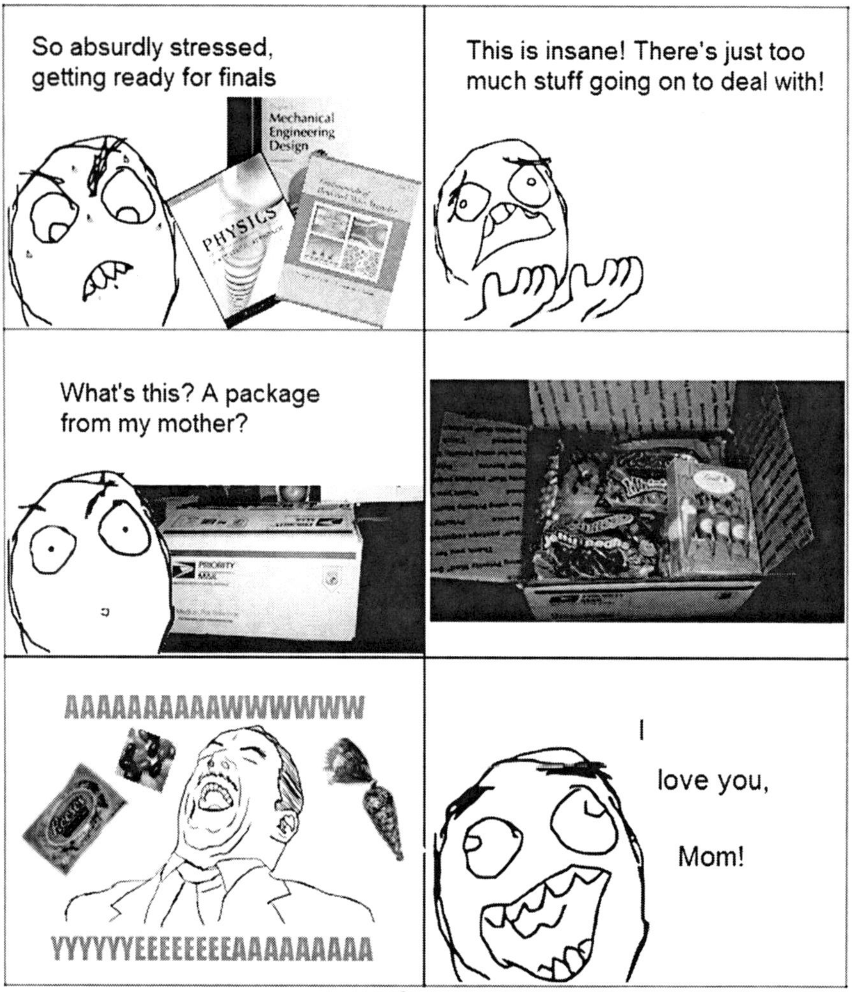
So absurdly stressed, getting ready for finals
This is insane! There's just too much stuff going on to deal with!
What's this? A package from my mother?
AAAAAAAAAWWWWWW
YYYYYYEEEEEEEEAAAAAAAAA
I love you, Mom!

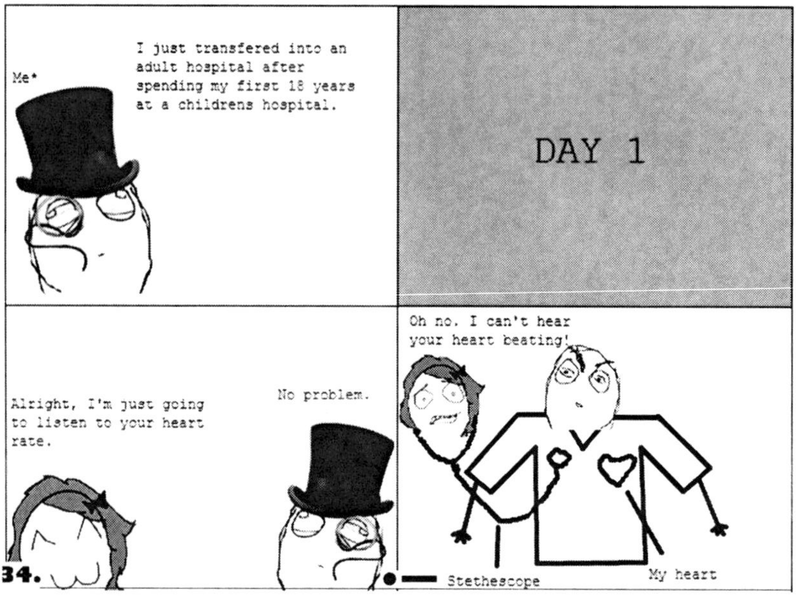
Me*
I just transfered into an adult hospital after spending my first 18 years at a childrens hospital.
DAY 1
Alright, I'm just going to listen to your heart rate.
No problem.
Oh no. I can't hear your heart beating!
Stethescope
My heart

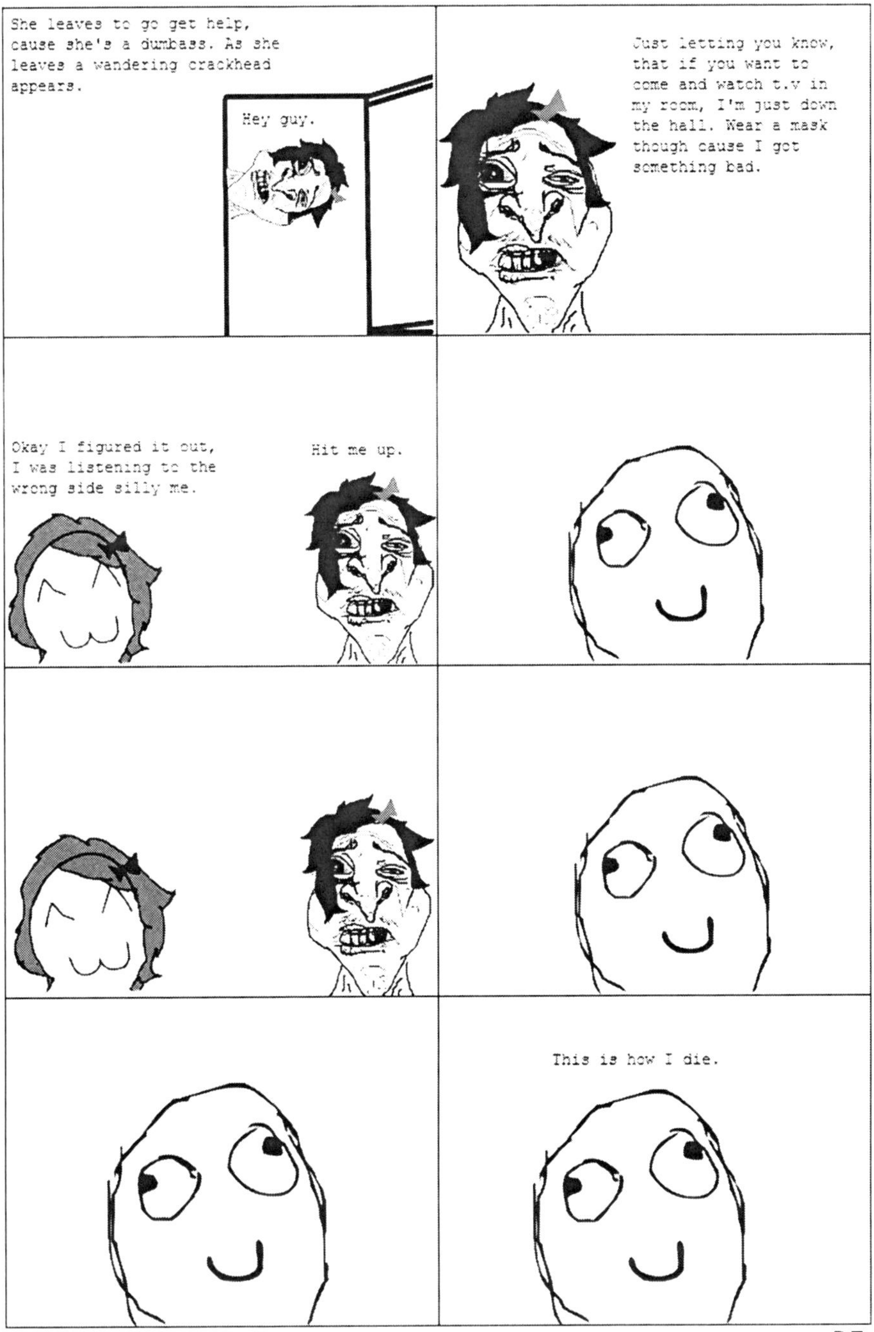

She leaves to go get help, cause she's a dumbass. As she leaves a wandering crackhead appears.
Hey guy.
Just letting you know, that if you want to come and watch t.v in my room, I'm just down the hall. Wear a mask though cause I got something bad.
Okay I figured it out, I was listening to the wrong side silly me.
Hit me up.
This is how I die.

Searching through TFINO.com funny picture thread
sees something
POKER FACE

So every guy I've been with has always wanted to cum on my face for his birthday gift
That's funny but I have no interest in cumming on your face, love.
but but..
My boyfriend and I on his birthday

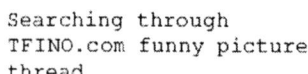

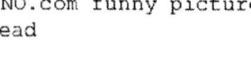

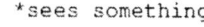

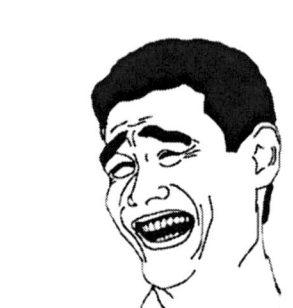

it's fine, I'm not going to cum on your face...
but...you're the only guy I'm willing to let do this...
It's okay. Really, it's Fine.
party hats off
No. Cum on my face.
15 minutes go by with me screaming for him to come on my face, Until....
Herp? What's this about coming?
Boyfriend's back pocket dialed someone
Current Call: MOM
Duration: 00:15:00
hangs up phone
POKER FACE
His mom knows I want her son's seed all over my FACE!

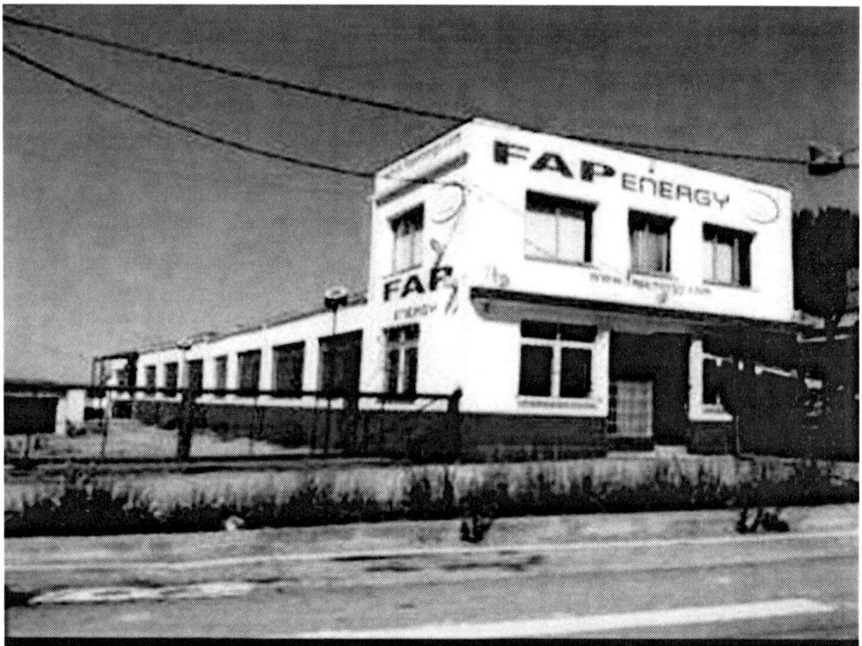
FAP ENERGY
FAP
ENERGY

Inside the building

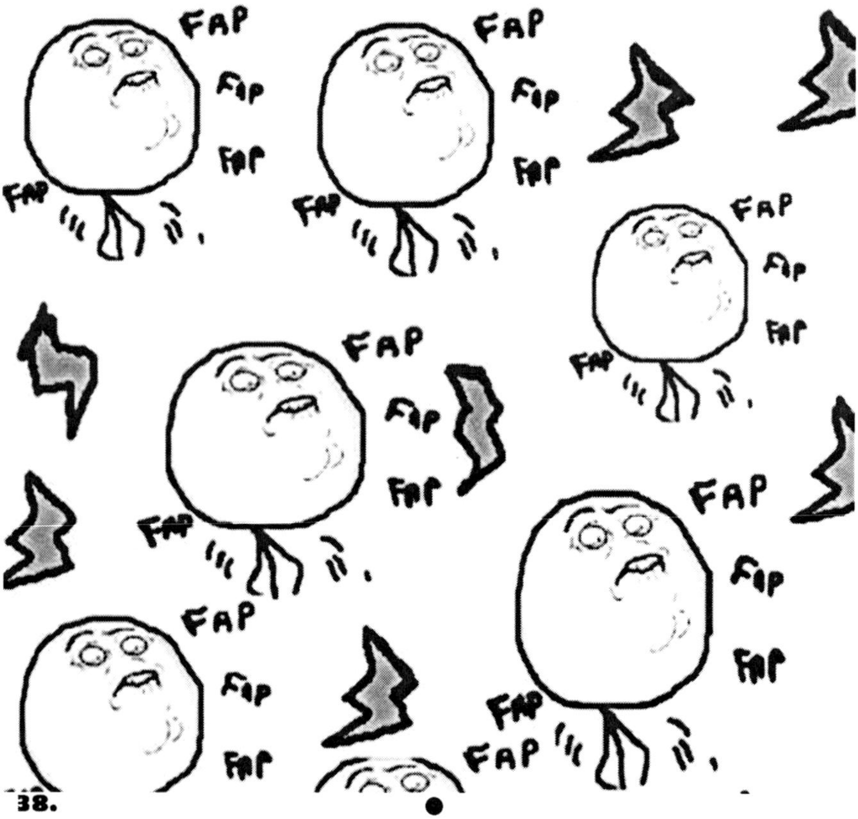
FAP
FAP
FAP
FAP
FAP
FAP
FAP
FAP
FAP
FAP
FAP
FAP
FAP
FAP
FAP
FAP
FAP
FAP
FAP
FAP
FAP
FAP
FAP
FAP
FAP
FAP

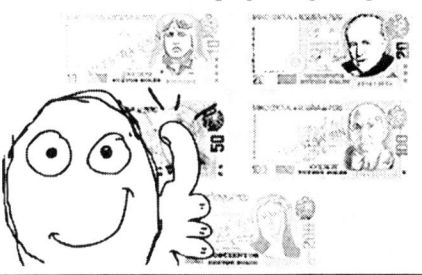

Going on a trip to Peru to help some impoverished people.	**I get there and realize my Spanish is terrible.** "YO HABLO ME GUSTA ESPANOL"
Local girl decides to follow me around and help me translate! "He ask, when will you sleep?" "que?" "cuando vas a la cama?"	**One night I show her and some other locals how to make paper ninja stars.**
They loved them!!	**I wanted to thank her at the end of the trip, so I figured I would give her the rest of my spending money.**
But I was told that we're not supposed to give money to the people there. "If you give money to one, you have to give money to all..."	**Devised clever plan to hide the rest of my spending money in a ninja star.** I'll just fold the money, and then it should fit...

39.

As I'm leaving, she's saying goodbye with a horde of people. So I throw the paper ninja star at her.	I look back as we're driving away, and notice that she has found the cash. She freaks out, smiles, waves, smiles, waves... FUCK YEA
Designing a derp at work	I HAVENT SAVED IN HOURS
Saving	Saving
Saving	

40.

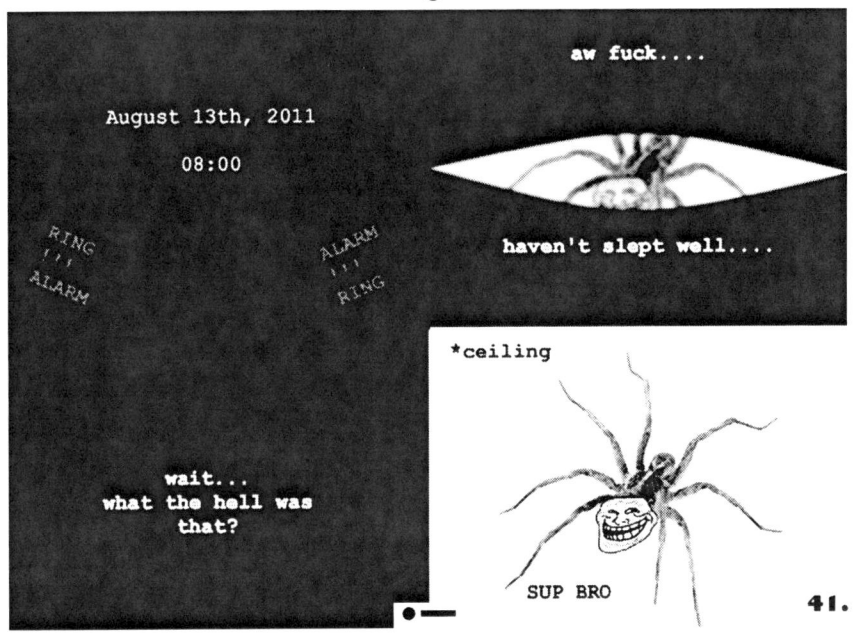

My friend and I playing Final Fantasy 2 for SNES many years ago

Why are you scrolling through the text so fast?

The story is boring, why do they put so much talking in it? I wanna kill stuff

It's a role playing game, the story is 75% of the game.

What's a Role Playing Game?

This is a stupid game I'm gonna put Shaq-Fu back in.

August 13th, 2011
08:00

RING!!! ALARM
ALARM!!! RING

wait... what the hell was that?

aw fuck....

haven't slept well....

*ceiling

SUP BRO

41.

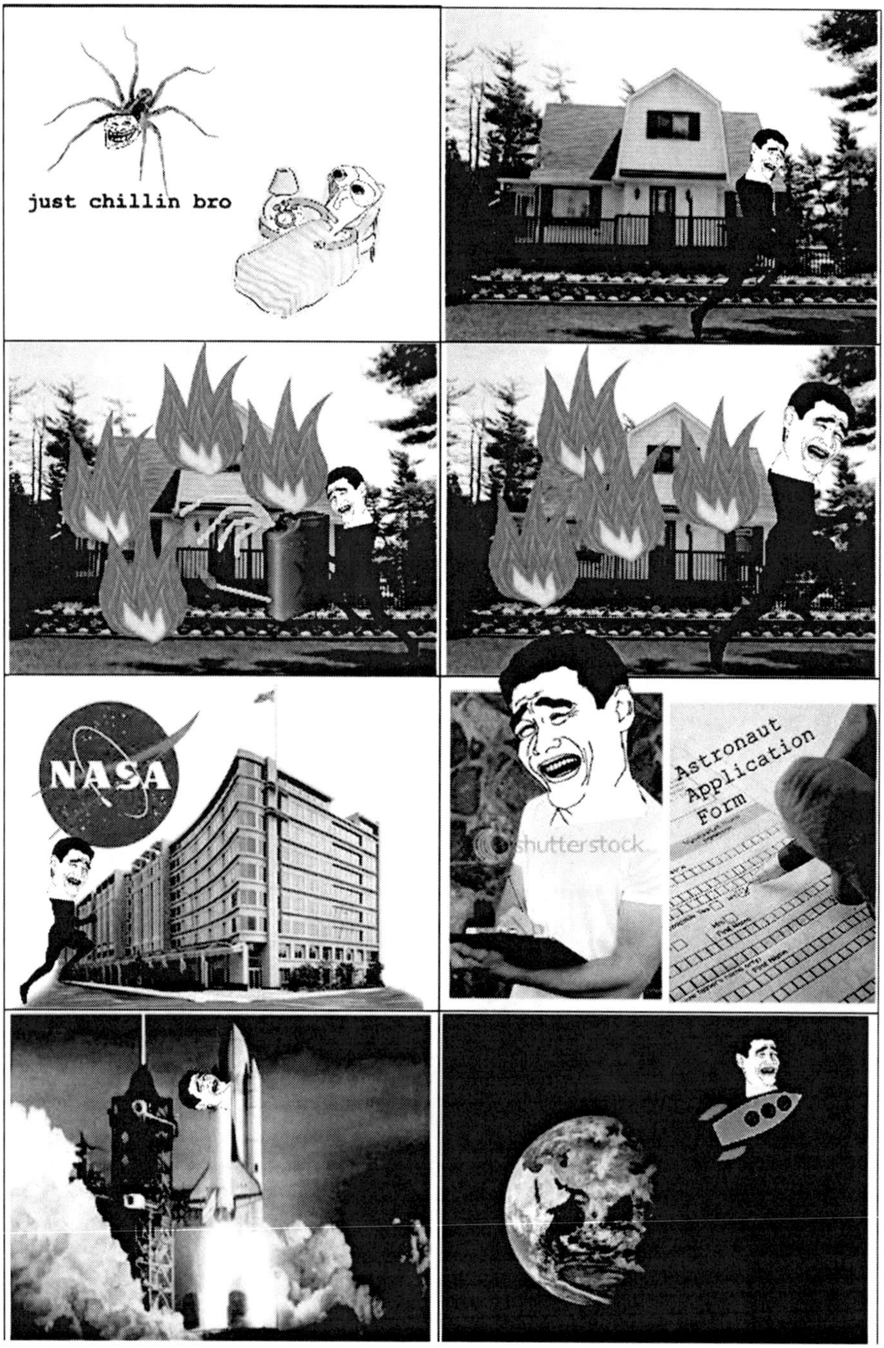
just chillin bro
NASA
shutterstock
Astronaut Application Form

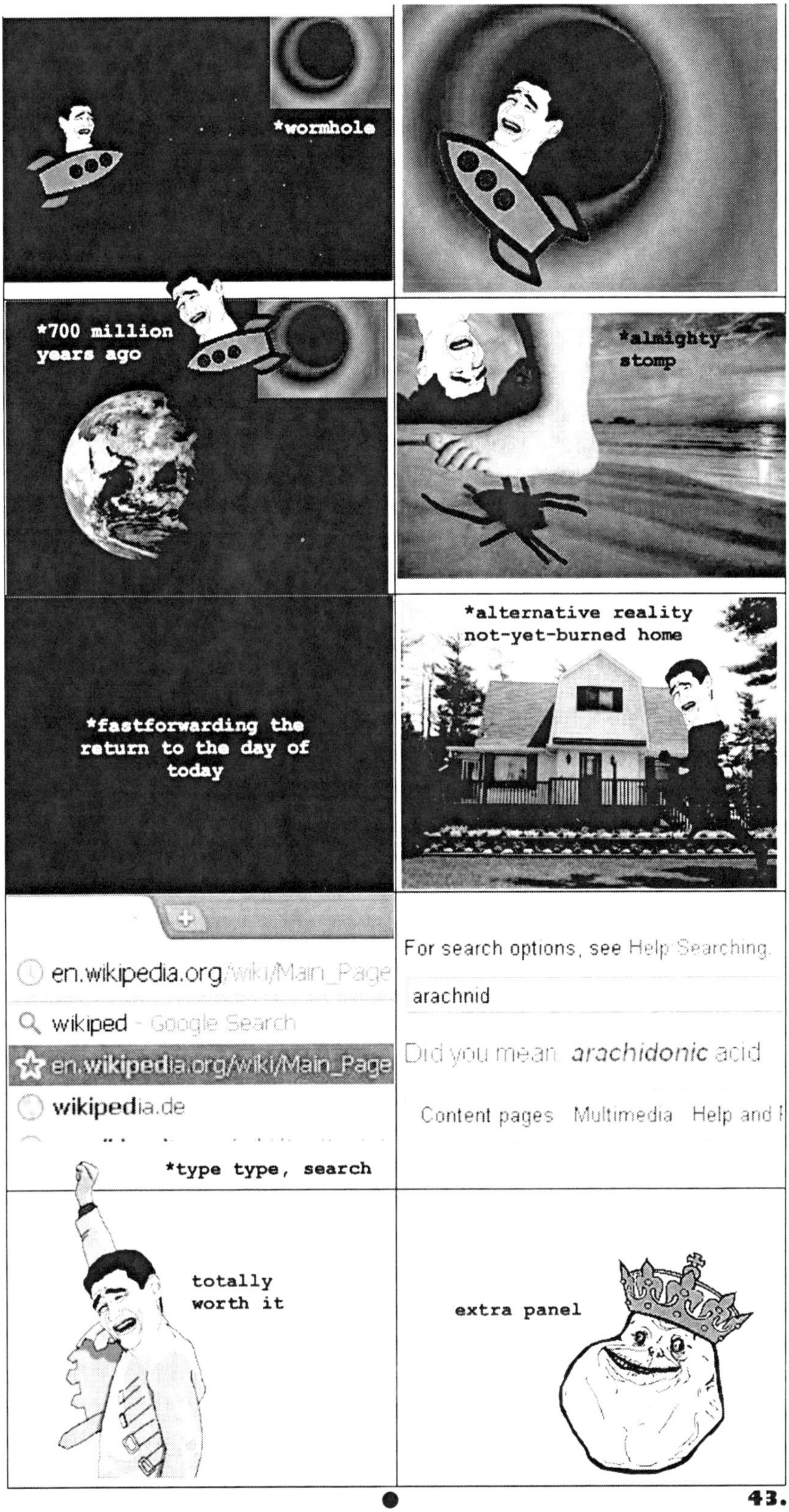
*wormhole
*700 million years ago
*almighty stomp
*fastforwarding the return to the day of today
*alternative reality not-yet-burned home
en.wikipedia.org/wiki/Main_Page
wikiped - Google Search
en.wikipedia.org/wiki/Main_Page
wikipedia.de
*type type, search
For search options, see Help:Searching.
arachnid
Did you mean: arachidonic acid
Content pages Multimedia Help and
totally worth it
extra panel

Rainy again?
It's been like
this over a week
now...
But I have to
go to class
and I don't have
an umbrella!

Me giving 5' 90 lb wife coffee for the first time
How do you feel baby?
*twitch
SCREAM ABOUT
ALL THE THINGS
RUN
ALL THE ERRANDS
HUG
ALL THE PUPPIES
SEX
ALL THE HUSBAND
ONE MINUTE THIRTY SEVEN SECONDS LATER...
zzzzzzzz

~le girlfriend and me~
Hey babe, look!
That guy over there
looks a lot like you
Hm... Where?
~le ugliest guy on the Earth~
C'mon Derpina,
are you serious?
Of course I am!
Okay

le flirting with a girl
So do you like the
beatles?
Are you kidding me...
Bugs are GROSS!!!

..le mad scientist woman working away on brilliant invention..
BEHOLD! I have created a mind reader hat capable of tuning into FM signals from the male brain!!
I shall use this device to learn all the secrets of the male gender..all their fears, their deepest, darkest, innermost thoughts..
THE WORLD SHALL BE MINNEEE!!! MUHAHAHAHAHA!! MUAHAHAHAHA!!!
..now must test apparatus on unsuspecting male subject..
Le bf
I'm hungry

Think I want something with like some cheese on it..
Can we order a pizza?
..This device is fucking worthless.
Boobs

*le eating olives
OLIV

Making Le bagel bites, microwaving for 3 minutes	Finally done! I'm starving! *Beep Beep Beeeeep*
Looking at instructions... Let bagels stand for 1 minute before serving no matter how much your kids beg!	

|  Just washing my hands after using the library's restroom at school... | Suddenly, I notice a man walk out of a stall and proceed to wash his hands next to me... |

49.

Um, you do realize that this is the woman's restroom, right?
I AM a woman.
POKER FACE
NOTHING TO DO HERE

*Just browsing reddit not doing anything special
OH MY GOD ITS HUGE COME KILL IT!
KILL IT!!!
Don't worry I got this
*le napkin
Today you tomorrow me
*months later sleeping in bed
I heard a thumd go check it out
alright

Put your hands up!!

What just happened?

Son. You need to stop playing those games.

But they're fun!

I don't see how they are fun.

Here. Play it dad!

One Eternity Later

You been playing my game for weeks. Let me play!

Shut up child! I need to get all the different colored yoshis.

"Did you want penis on that?"

Me derping at the ice cream store

"What?"

le customer

"I said 'Do you want peanuts on that?'"

"Oh...Ummm no thanks"

I actually did say penis!

At the mall with GF and we go to GameStop.

GF wanders off in the store while I'm looking at GBA games, continue looking at games.

52.

See a short person step up beside me in my peripheral vision, think it's my wife and put my arm around her side
And then I say:
"After this, I need to go to the pharmacy. We're out of flavored condoms. we need to buy the ones you like"
mfw I look over and it's a little girl who's like 10, looking up at me confused
POKER FACE
"WHOA. Uhh... Sorry."
POKER FACE
Let go and hurry away
Grab GF, gtfo the store
Notice girl talking to her mom and pointing at me on the way out.
True Story

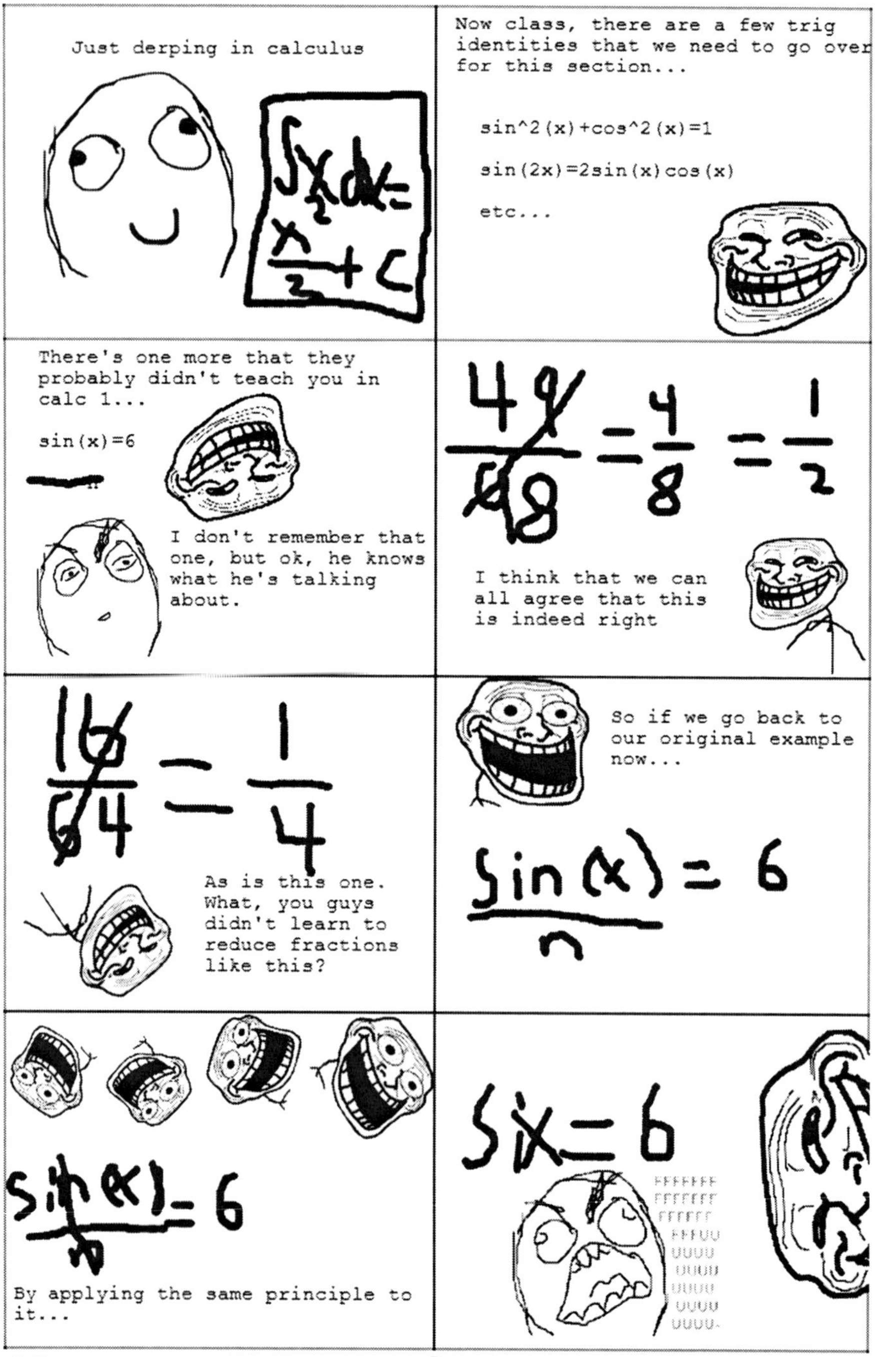

Just derping in calculus

$$\int \frac{x}{2} dx = \frac{x^2}{2} + C$$

Now class, there are a few trig identities that we need to go over for this section...

$sin^2(x) + cos^2(x) = 1$

$sin(2x) = 2sin(x)cos(x)$

etc...

There's one more that they probably didn't teach you in calc 1...

$sin(x) = 6$

I don't remember that one, but ok, he knows what he's talking about.

$$\frac{4\cancel{y}}{\cancel{d}8} = \frac{4}{8} = \frac{1}{2}$$

I think that we can all agree that this is indeed right

$$\frac{1\cancel{6}}{\cancel{6}4} = \frac{1}{4}$$

As is this one. What, you guys didn't learn to reduce fractions like this?

So if we go back to our original example now...

$$\frac{sin(x)}{n} = 6$$

$$\frac{\cancel{sin}(x)}{\cancel{n}} = 6$$

By applying the same principle to it...

$six = 6$

FFFFFFF
FFFFFFF
FFFFFF
FFFUU
UUUU
UUUU
UUUU
UUUU-

54.

le making wedding invitations with fiance's hot sister

I know you're marrying my sister, but I can't resist you any longer. If you want to have one more wild time before marriage, meet me in my room.

heads to front door

le wild family appears

LOL
LOL
LOL

You passed the test! I knew you were the right man to marry my daughter!

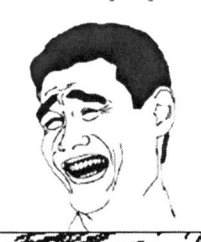

Always keep your condoms in the car.

PARENTS GENERATION
OUR GENERATION
woo hoo, it's free love! go have sex and enjoy it!
DON'T FUCK ANYBODY OR YOU GET AIDS AND DIE
Okay
My job pays for the entire family which means that my wife doesn't have to work and can spend time raising the kids
GET A THIRD JOB SO WE CAN PAY THIS MONTHS BILLS
Okay
I do say, Mrs Prime Minister, economic times are good.
SPEND
ALL THE MONEY
THERE'S NO FUCKING MONEY LEFT AND THE ECONOMY IS SHIT, YOU'RE GOING TO HAVE TO WORK SOME SHIT JOB FOR YEARS EVEN THOUGH YOU HAVE A DEGREE AND A GREAT RESUME
Okay

Yeah, I can afford this house and mortgage reasonably, let me just sign the lease!	Shitty two bedroom house outside of the town? That'll be £350,000
	Okay

Derping around Wikipedia, reading some creepy articles when suddenly...

This guy appears!

Honey would you mind holding the baby?	Hey there little guy. Let's play the catching game!

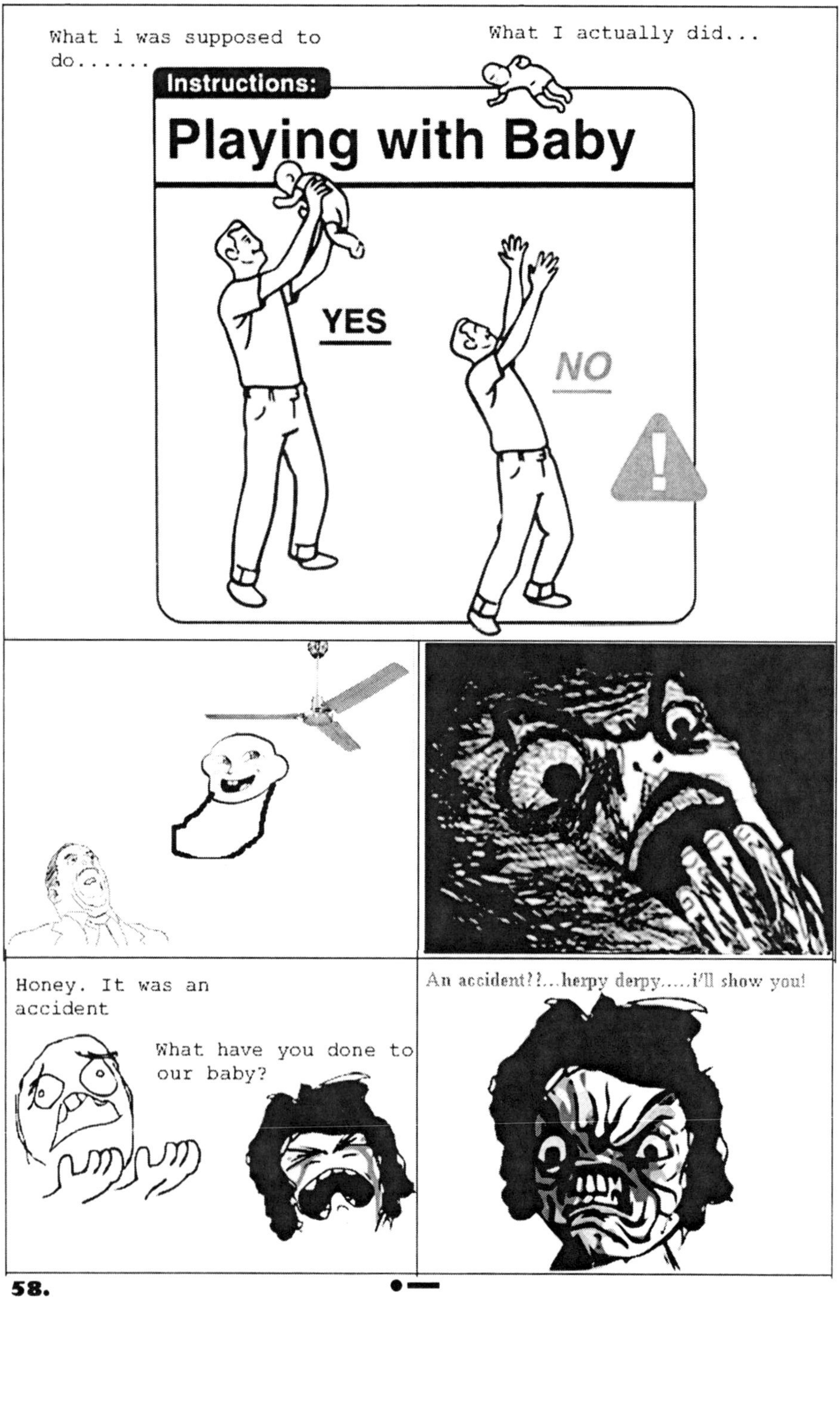
What i was supposed to do......
What I actually did...
Instructions:
Playing with Baby
YES
NO
Honey. It was an accident
What have you done to our baby?
An accident??...herpy derpy.....i'll show you!

How to you plead to the court Mr.Derp?
Guilty your honour, but it was just an accident!
In that case you will be sentenced to DEATH...
Honey would you mind holding the baby?

Time to get up for school, Derp!
DERP ARE YOU GETTING UP????

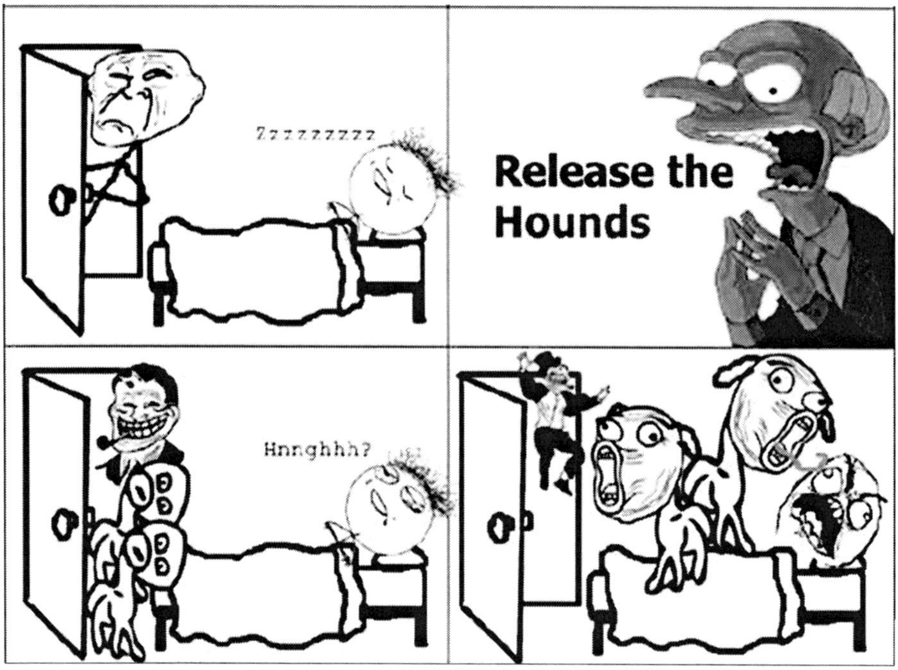
Zzzzzzzzz
Release the Hounds
Hnnghhh?

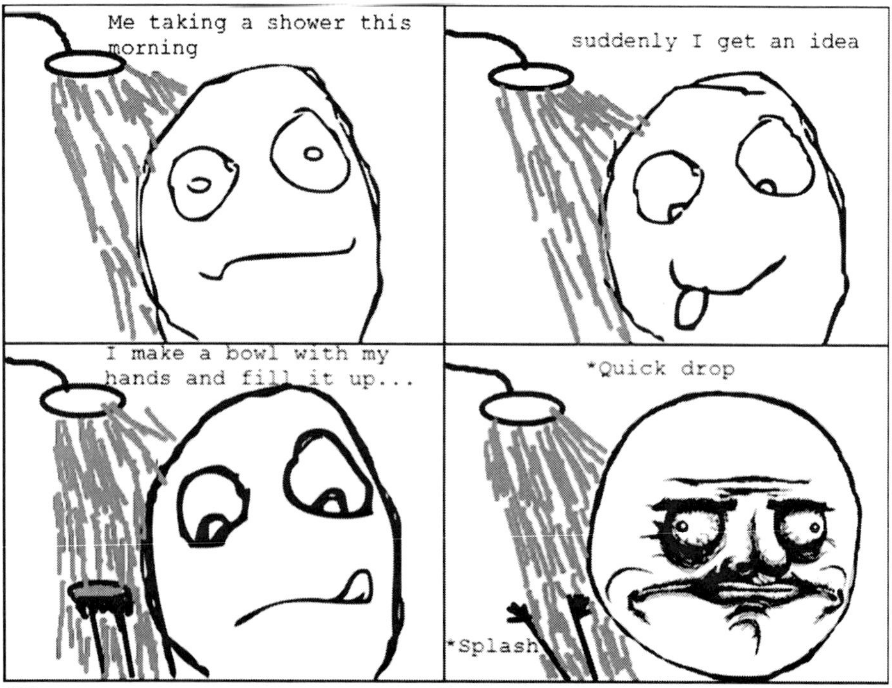
Me taking a shower this morning
suddenly I get an idea
I make a bowl with my hands and fill it up...
*Quick drop
*Splash

le me sitting in the subway
train brakes. me has to leave here
~ eeeeeeeeek ~
using inertia to stand up
I am the master of physics

*le purr
*le purr
*le purr

*Le me, on my second date with Derpina. And it's going really well. We met online, and we hit it off right away. Futurama! Ninja Turtles Blah blah blah	*IAMA workaholic, so I don't go out on dates a lot. She's really smart, which is a huge + for me. *Awesome that its going so well. I hope this turns into something
*The end of dinner comes. And she drops the bomb.	*The entire date she had been texting on and off. a little rude, but its 2011, so I don't mind. Takka takka takka
*I'm a dominatrix. *oh?	*I got into it because I met my master. Who taught me everything I know, and now I do it professionally as a side gig.
*Me trying to be modern and evolved and excepting of this *So what kind of stuff do you do? BAD POKER FACE	* Ya know the typical BDSM stuff, I like to be really dominant and agressive. *But I'll do cattle prods, handcuffs, tying up, whipping. Straight guy on straight guy.

62.

Straight guy... ...On Straight guy?	Yeah it's where straight guys have fantasies about being raped so I fascilitate that. Or a lot of times I'll just rape them myself with a dildo.
	*My master is actually my boyfriend. We broke up, so I went on a date with you. But now we're back together. But he wants me to date you because it makes him jealous. Takka takka takka
	* She stands up *Anyways, I got to go. There's a guy tied up at my house. I left him there to come on this date. I should probably go check on him.
*Sorry 'bout all the texting. I've been talking to my master. He's super hard so I have to go. *Shows me pic she just got.	

me playing Halo: Reach

When suddenly, a wild text message from my depressed friend who really likes me appears

Her: im so drunk and i took so many meds

Me: What meds?

Her: Prozac, ativan, hydroxictine.. all of them :P

Me: What the fuck?

I was pretty sure she was fucking with me but I didn't want to take any chances so I called the cops to check on her.

(p.s. it took me fucking forever to figure out how to reach police via text since i'm hearing impaired, im still mad about this)

OMG U CALLED THE COPS ILL NEVER FORGIVE U I WASNT GONNA KILL MYSELF MY SISTER IS HERE WITH ME U WORRY ABOUT ME TOO MUCH UR MAKING THINGS WORSE IM IN LOVE WITH U AND NOW MY SISTER IS PISSED AN U THINK UR HELPING BUT UR NOT THIS IS A FUCKIN DISASTER OMG I DONT WANT TO EVER TALK TO U AGAIN I HATE U NEVER EVER TRY TO CONTACT ME EVER AGAIN

Turns out, she was hoping I'd somehow tell her I'm in love with her (which I'm not) if she threatened suicide.

Well, obviously I don't fuck around with bullshit. If any one thinks this is a good idea then go fuck yourself.

bitch made me quit a good match

RUSSIA   GERMANY

JAPAN    CHINA

FRANCE 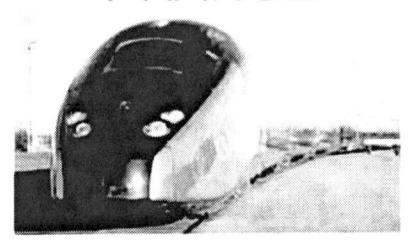   United States

PUT AMERICANS BACK TO WORK AND IMPROVE OUR ECONOMY AT THE SAME TIME

☞ **Rebuild Our Antique Infrastructure** ☜

Trick or treat Mrs. Robinson.

Hey kids. Wait a minute, forever alone?

Yes, me. I`m dressed like a person who has friends.

~le fake friends~

15 year old me
FAP
Man i think i am addicted to porn, i need to fix that
FAP
FAP
FAP
Guess i will block 18+ stuff in my internet explorer, and put a random password so i dont unblock it in the future
Internet explorer options
Block Adult content
Password
Internet explorer options
Block Adult content
Password ************
Type random password without looking
De enter
Passowrd successfully changed
What
Have I
Done
NOOOOOO!!

Desesperate try to figure out password by positioning the fingers on the same buttons as before.

tec
 tec
  tec
   tec
    enter

Correct password ✓

Me, last night at a halloween party dressed as a giant bird.

Girl dressed as a bee on the dance floor.

Excuse me. Did your mother ever tell you about the birds and the bees?

Come on, bitch! That was
sort of funny!

*morning routine, taking glasses off to put in contacts
UGH!These are disgusting!
*toss like a boss
*new contacts
pop
pop
POKER FACE
SWEET JEEZ-IT THESE FEEL HEAVENLY

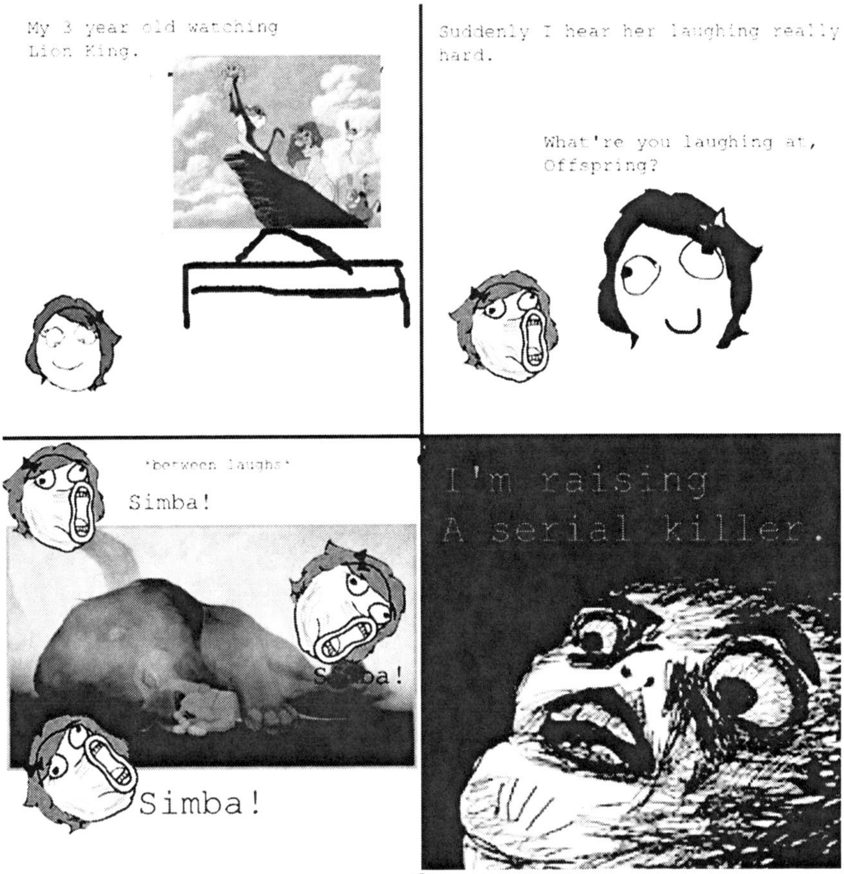
My 3 year old watching Lion King.
Suddenly I hear her laughing really hard.
What're you laughing at, Offspring?
between laughs
Simba!
Simba!
I'm raising A serial killer.

*me watching spongebob on tv
*The episode mentions and shows boat mobiles several times
I wonder where all these boat mobiles com from? Do they have a factory?

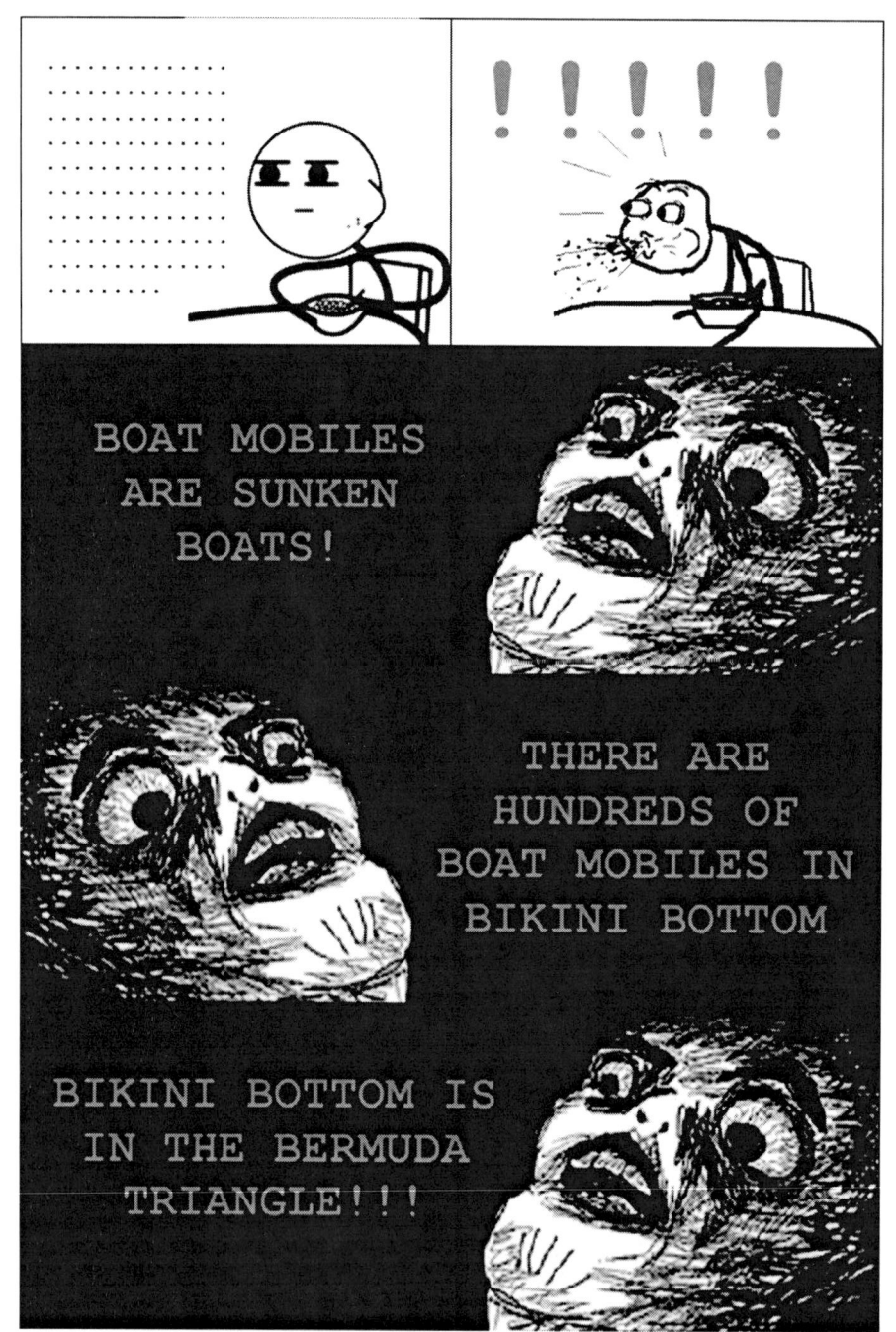

BOAT MOBILES ARE SUNKEN BOATS!

THERE ARE HUNDREDS OF BOAT MOBILES IN BIKINI BOTTOM

BIKINI BOTTOM IS IN THE BERMUDA TRIANGLE!!!

fresh out of
a morning
shower
need some q-tips for my
ears, but none in my
bathroom.
hey dad, do
you have any-?
dad has pokemon on in his room?
NOT BAD

Me sitting in library when i see
a hot female appear.
Im awkward around girls. How
should i start the conversation.

I should start by saying how nice the weather is.	Hey Derpina... how are weather?
POKER FACE	
 le moi and le gf having intense le sexytimes le gf le moi	When suddenly.... Derp if i dont eat im going to pass out, you are ruining me

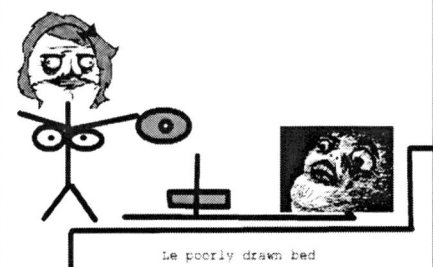

So le gf disappears downstairs and returns with two strawberry donuts... Get on your back... NOW YOU SEXY DERP!!! Le poorly drawn donut	I then lay on my back and le gf places le donuts on my cock Le poorly drawn bed
Le gf begins to eat the dohnuts off my cock...	And she didnt stop until they were both all gone..

And it was on that day that i became the Donut King

me out shopping notice batman socks "What is the deal with this ribbon?"

OMG the socks have CAPES!

NANANANANANANA
NANANANANANANA
NANANANANANANA
NANANANANANANA
NANANANANANANA
NANANANANANANA
NANANANANANANA

BATSOCKS

Me, walking to class

Girl that I kind of know approches, but I'm not sure if I should say Hi

Hey!

I HAVE A GIRLFRIEND!!!

*me and le fiancee derpin' around at the pharmacy.

We pick out a lube we'll both enjoy, and she walks off.

On the way to check out, she hands me 4 boxes of tissues that are on sale, then disappears to look at stuffed animals.

I reach the counter and place the lube and tissues down. My fiancee is nowhere in sight.

"Big Plans?"

"The tissues are for my fiancee."

She just wanted to play with the stuffed animals.

Why are you looking at me like that?

Bambi's mother death scene	My reaction every time:
Pikachu's tears.	My reaction every time:
..Long Live the king.	My reaction every time:

Panel 1
Hey, Dad! I wanna be a cowboy this halloween!

4 year old me

Panel 2
Of Course! I'll go buy the costume right now!

Panel 3
Okay

Panel 4
True Story

"Okay, we're going to take a sample of your blood to make sure you have enough iron."
le me, about to donate blood
pricks finger and samples blood
"Let's see...you need 12.1g/dL to donate and you have..woah! 14.3, plenty of iron!

le little sister commandeers the tv to watch cartoons
tv: Are you ready kids? AYE AYE CAPTAIN!I can't hear you!
AYE AYE CAPTAIN!
Outside:
Okay I guess I might as well watch with you...
POKER FACE
Inside:
Oh boy!Oh boy!Oh boy!Oh boy!Oh boy!Oh boy!Oh boy!Oh boy!

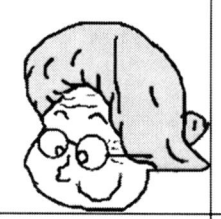

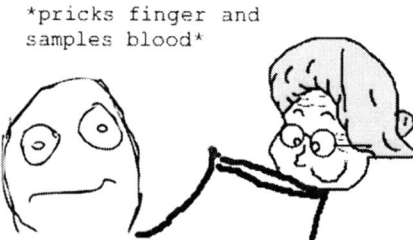

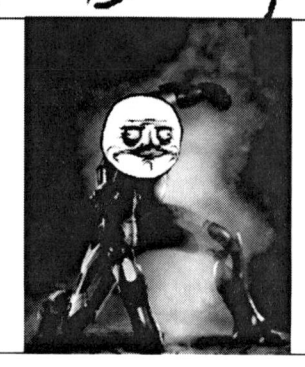

*le me, browsing imgur

*When suddenly, a wild ad appears

What?

ARE YOU TOO OLD TO GO BACK TO SCHOOL?

What the fuck is that?

Le me Le coworker Working like underpaid slaves	Just like any bored 19 year olds we start casual conversation "So who did you lose you V card to?"
"Yeah I lost it to my Aunt when I was 14"	
POKER FACE "Actually, the only women I had sex with were my three aunts"	**POKER FACE** "I don't count one of them though. I just fucked her to get back at my uncle for cheating on her"

WHAT IN THE FUCK?

Ha, I've already killed 3!
How many have you killed, Legolas?
42

*le moi in class beside a girl i like
*awesomely drawn desks.
*she says "hi"
*i say the first thing that comes in mind...
"i like trains!"

HOW I FEEL WHEN I FIRST GET A GIRLFRIEND:

HANG OUT ALL OF THE TIME

HOW I FEEL AFTER 1 YEAR OR SO WITH A GIRL:

Y U NO LEAVE ME THE FUCK ALONE!?!?!?!

Me, working for a health insurance company as a sales agent in their call center

Derp, would you mind doing a few recordings for our automated system?

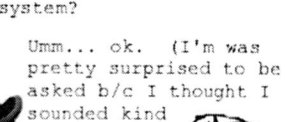

Umm... ok. (I'm was pretty surprised to be asked b/c I thought I sounded kind of nasally)

*Boss

So there I am, recording the entire everything for my company's call center.

"For English, press 1. Para llamada en Espanol, marque el numero dos..."

It took hours, but I was finally finished.

My company has about 1,000 employees, but I barely knew anyone. One day a company wide email is sent thanking me for the recordings and people start recognizing me.
"Hey, you're the voice dude"
"How's the voice?"
Now people I have never seen before know me as "the voice"
"The Voice"
"Yo, Voice!"
"Hey Voice"
"Sup Voice?"
I AM THE VOICE
I AM METATRON

*le me and girlfriend getting it on in her car (in semi-abandoned parking lot)
FAP
FAP
FAP
FAP
*I look out the window and notice there is a guy staring at us only a few cars away
NO ME GUSTA
ACTUALLY...

*I keep going thinking the guy will leave soon enough
*he stays for another 15 mintues....
*He finally leaves
"There was a guy in the car next to us watching us the whole time...."
BAD POKER FACE
"ME GUSTA"

AT A BBQ
Hey dad!
Can you
toast the buns
for the burgers?
TO THE BUNS!

Le suicide by
Hanging.
(The guy's dead and
still swinging in
the breeze.)
Buddy of dead guy
Le me
I just talked to him last
night! He seemed to be in
a great mood! I don't
understand why he seemed
so happy?
People who hang themselves are
very depressed. When they've
made up their mind, they actually
may feel better and seem happy.
But they're motivated and you
can't stop them. I'm sorry you
have to see him this way.
I'm going to cut him down.
I'm sorry, I can't let you
do that.
We have to wait for the
Coroner to swing by. I'll
hang around until he gets
here.

BAD POKER FACE

LOL

What? Puns are funny okay? We both laughed, broke the tension and this is a good example of dark humour. Have you ever seen a dead guy who hung himself? It's fucked up shit. Humour is one way to deal with it.

/* 1st year at job, had 1 week of sick time but never got sick, so it expired.*/

/* My co-workers, and supervisors heard that I didn't use my time...*/

"But that was your time to use!"

"It's part of your compensation!"

"Well, I guess this year I'll be sure to use my time."

"But I'll space my days out, and only take off when there's not a lot of work to do."

88.

/* May 15 */

/* July 22 */

/* Fast-forward to 2-year performance review */

"You're doing a fine job, Derp. But we noticed that you've been out a lot this year. Please try to work on that."

le lounging on Saturday morning

ME

on my first day off in 5 weeks.

When suddenly a wild girlfriend appears...

Hey herp can you go pick up some eggs and milk?

89.

But Derpette, it's my first day off in forever...
Too bad, I'm making breakfast and I need eggs and milk!
If I go, do I get le sexy times?
Sure!
Go to store like a boss...
HATERS GONNA HATE
Get le sexy times...
I was going to go to the store for you anyway!

How people are supposed to get on/off the train

How people actually get on/off the train

Playing megaman 5

Le Final Boss!

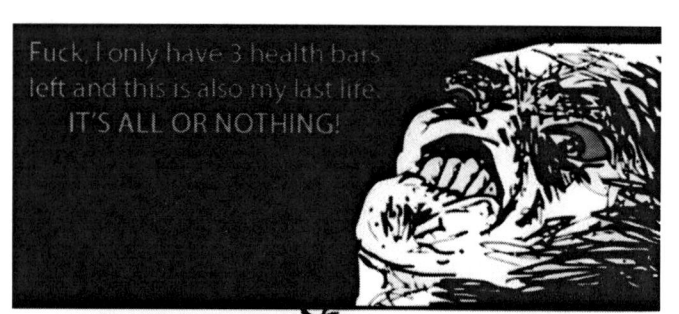

Fuck, I only have 3 health bars left and this is also my last life.
IT'S ALL OR NOTHING!

Take this you asshole.
The final shot....

simultaneous death

GAME OVER

at university sexual education seminar, asking and answer question about sex. we are all 18+ year olds.
le me
le roommate
random dormmate raises her hand to ask a question.
"why yes, derpette, what is your question?"
le instructor
"UH YEAH I HEARD THAT IF YOU ARE PREGNANT AND HAVE SEX YOU CAN GET DOUBLE PREGNANT."
"...Did you take sex ed in high school?"
"NO. SEX ED ENCOURAGES TEENAGERS TO HAVE SEX!!! ONLY ABSTINENCE WORKS!!!!!!"
FUCK THIS GENERATION

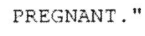

"Hey, Derp. I wanted to let you know that I'm sleeping at a friend's room tonight since she doesn't feel well, and she said you can come too!"

Hm.. If I come over that means I can..

Sleep in the bed with two girls!

"Sure, I'll come over!"

"Alright, I'll tell her!"

WHAT I EXPECTED SLEEPING WITH TWO GIRLS WOULD BE LIKE:

WHAT ACTUALLY HAPPENED:

*me, derping aroud when I was little
*I had just recently lost a tooth
When suddenly, a wild juice box appears
*le straw fits perfectly between teeth
ME GUSTA
crazy pills LOL
Taking my antidepressants before bed
"That didn't taste/feel like my celexa.."

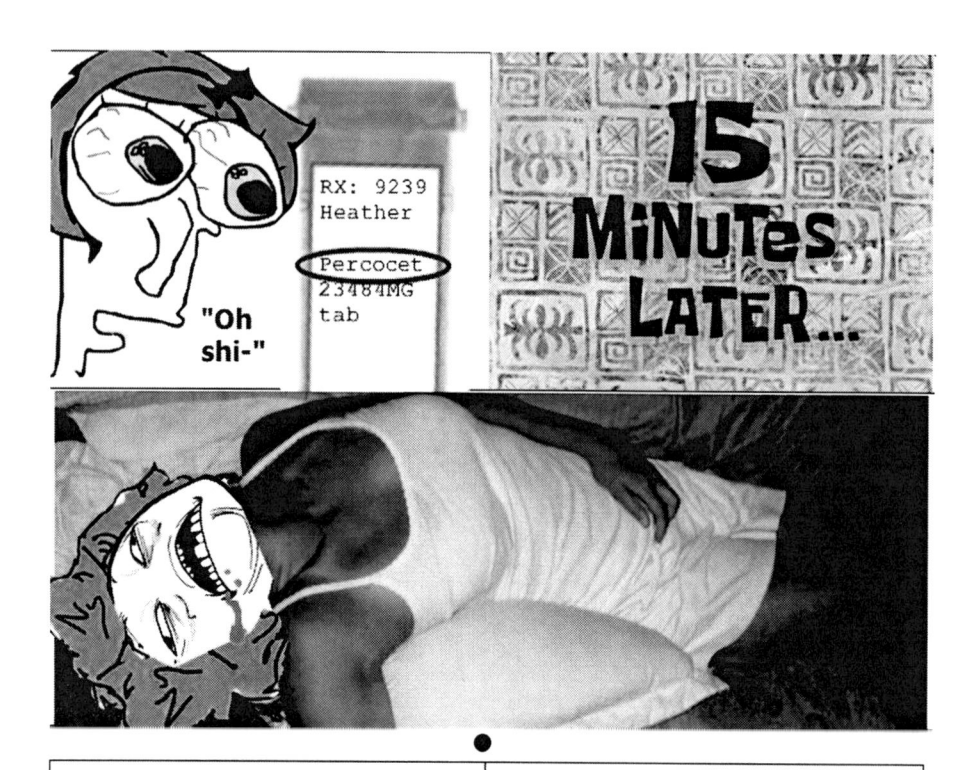

"Oh shi-"

RX: 9239
Heather
Percocet
23484MG
tab

15 MiNuTeS LATeR...

Me, talking to my future brother-in-law about the new 55" TV my fiance and I got.

*Me   *Him

"The picture is amazing! Movies look like they're in the room with you!"

"I agree! Everything on here looks great!"

"I'm definetly going to buy some blu-ray pornos"

"I want to borrow that after you!"

I then get up and start walking to the kitchen, but I shout back at him...

96.

Panel 1
I CAN'T WAIT TO SEE SOME HIGH-DEF TITTIES!!!

Panel 2
"Corysgro, my parents are here..."

Kitchen

*Fiance

*Soon-to-be in-laws

Panel 3
POKER FACE

Panel 4
"Uh.... Hi"

BAD POKER FACE

Panel 5
And none of us ever spoke of it again.

Panel 6
goodnight family and random house guest!

*me

Panel 7
too awake to sleep, I decided to rummage through old things in my room

what's this?

Pooooot

POOOOOOT
PFfffTTT
poot poot

after many farts, I remember that the houseguest is staying across the hall and definitely heard everything.

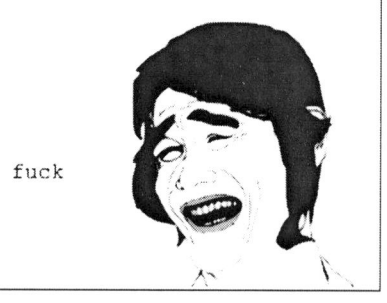

fuck

sorry but i don't think i can put this on the showcase.

*me in art class.

well... its too sexual.

what?? why??

98.

Oh okay that makes sense..
Wait a second..
I DREW A JELLYFISH.

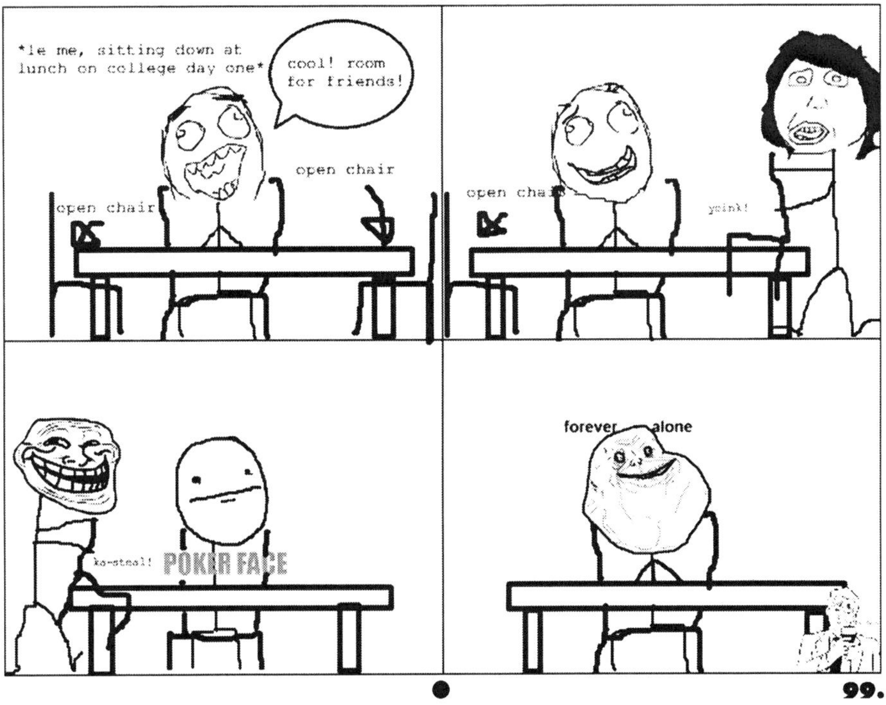
le me, sitting down at lunch on college day one
cool! room for friends!
open chair
open chair
open chair
yoink!
ko-steal!
POKER FACE
forever alone

*le teacher.

Right class, we are going to be learning about sex education...

Okay, i'm going to be mature about this!

*le moi.

The main differences about boys and girls is that boys have penis.

BAD POKER FACE

LOL

She Said Penis!!!!!

Me and 5 other friends playing halo. My team is kicking ass

*kicking ass

*asses getting kicked

100.

Pissed because hes losing, one friend on the other team quits and starts beating it

FAP
FAP
FAP

he goes all the way until he finishes

WHY THE FUCK DID YOU JUST DO THAT??

*me, pretending im sick at age 8...

"Mom! I swear Im sick! My throat hurts!"

"Ok fine, you can stay home today"

101.

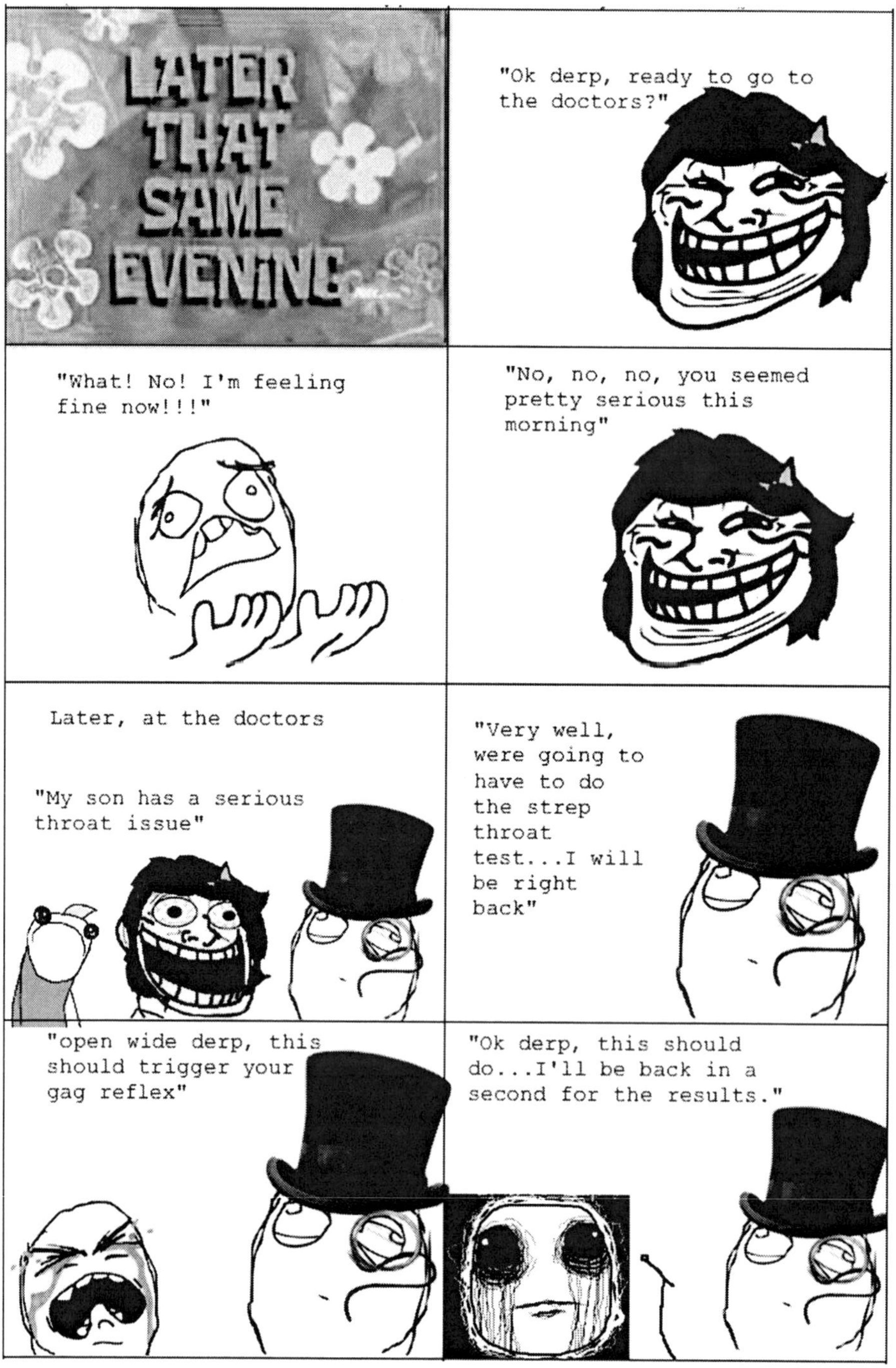
LATER THAT SAME EVENING
"Ok derp, ready to go to the doctors?"
"What! No! I'm feeling fine now!!!"
"No, no, no, you seemed pretty serious this morning"
Later, at the doctors
"My son has a serious throat issue"
"Very well, were going to have to do the strep throat test...I will be right back"
"open wide derp, this should trigger your gag reflex"
"Ok derp, this should do...I'll be back in a second for the results."

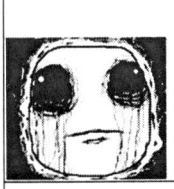

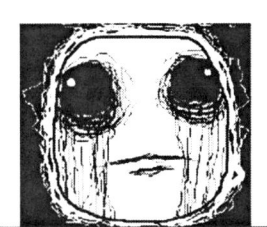

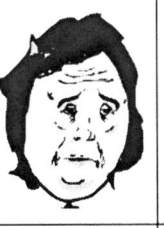

"Ok derp, do you promise never to fake sick again?"	And just as im about to confess...
"Well...the results came up positive, but its a very minor case..."	
While were just about to leave, the doctor walks over to me...	Hands me a lollipop and says..
"feel better kid..." *Le epic wink*	And then my mom apologized, told me I could stay home all week and I never saw that doctor again...

Me, washing dishes, with excellently drawn sink	*a spoon*
	FFFFFFF FFFFFFF FFFFFF FFFUU UUUU UUUU UUUU UUUU UUUU-

SEX ED
I have a question
What is "oral sex"?
Oral sex is umm.. when people umm.. talk in bed
POKER FACE
LATER...
Do you guys want to have oral sex?
THE NEXT DAY
How was your sleepover, son?
It was great mom. We had oral sex all night long.
OH GOD
WHY

Kids, put on your seatbelts-
I think someone is following mommy.
SOCCER MOM
Why did they pause the movie?!

*Little Me, derping around in the yard
Derp, can you shovel the walk for me?
*Le Mom

Yes Mom...
*Super packed sidewalk snow
I know! I can just run really fast and shovel it all at once!
*Running with a shovel like a boss
*Le crack in the sidewalk
Fuck.

Nutty, Fudge covered goodness

Crispy, sweet vanilla ice cream

Fudge Clump from God's own dessert tray

When I was younger, my brother and I would take showers together, no big deal.

One day, we thought of a really cool song and dance!

BUTT TO BUTT IS WHAT WE LOVE!
A B C D BUTT TO BUTT!
"MOMMMM COME HEAR OUR SONGGGG!!!"""
BUTT TO BUTT IS WHAT WE LOVE!
OH GOD
WHY

*a wild t-rex appears
POKER FACE
POKER FACE

Wait! His vision is based on movement!
He can't see us if we don't move!
Do...Not..Move...
¡Rawr!
...
Grrr...

...
...
POKER FACE
What kind of wizardry is this?

*me and younger brother, bathing together at young age
After bath...
You ready bro?
Always
AND NOW IT'S TIME FOR
THE DINGALING SHOW!

A ding-a-linga-ding-a-linga ding-a-linga-ding
strumming
actual lyrics
OH GOD OH GOD
WHY
*youngest sister looks in curiously
"...what...what are you guys doing?"
....dingaling show.
POKER FACE
POKER FACE
Oooh! Oooh! Can I play? I want to be an instrument! What instrument can I be?

a ding-a-linga-ding-a-linga-dinga
drums...drums drums
drums...drums... drums
OH GOD
OH GOD
WHY
*Le me,
walking somewhere
*My pocket,
full of change
*Clink
*Step

*me picking up my moms checks from her preschool like a boss
*tiny little preschoolers running around
POKER FACE
POKER FACE

taking a swim in the lake
when suddenly,
something
touches my foot
get me
the fuck
out of
here.

Me, playing tetris
I'm working my ass off,
when suddenly, a wild
perfect clear chance
appears

click
U mad bro?
FFFFFFF
FFFFFFF
FFFFFF
FFFUU
UUUU
UUUU
UUUU
UUUU
UUUU-

What can I get you for dessert?
Can I get some Vanilla Ice Cream with Gummy Bears?
Sorry, we're out of gummy bears...

WHAT. DID. YOU. JUST. SAY?
We may have some worms...
That is unacceptable!!
I will have my gummy bears!
Give me my gummy bears!
BITCH!
GIVE THEM TO ME!
HELP!!!!!
Then she starts having a seizure
Random Customer Get her to the floor and pin her down!

Legs
Arms
Head
The EMTs arrive
Thank you ladies, we got it from here.
And that's why I'm a little out of it right now. What did you say you wanted?

*me opening a picture on my phone
Hard to enjoy the pic.. Gotta turn my phone to the left!
*after a turn
FFFFFFF
FFFFFFF
FFFFFF
FFFUU
UUUU
UUUU
UUUU
UUUU
UUUU-

le me working fast food circa 2002
le head manager
Hi Derpette, I just wanted to commend you on your wonderful sandwich making skills
Why thank you for noticing.
You're faster, cleaner, and less wasteful than any of the other employees
Blah
Blah
Blah
Blah
explaining my methods and how they differ from what the other employees were doing...
But that's not how the employee handbook says you're supposed to do things
But you just complimented me on my methods. If I do things the old way I'll be slower and less efficient.
But your way is wrong. Please follow the handbook.
...and that's why she was a 40 year old fast food employee.

Masturbate ferociously	Sing as loud as possible
FAP FAP FAP	I'M SAILING AWAY!!!!
Piss everywhere	Breakdance randomly
Have sex	Direct action films
	...but then, out of NOWHERE, comes the evil DR. SHAMPOO to foil DUCKBERT from saving...

Rack up massive water bills

120.

Panel 1: *shopping at toys'r'derp
Wow, someone must have been a good boy this year!

Panel 2: Yeah... he's such a great kid.
You're such an awesome dad!

Panel 3: I don't have any kids. These toys are for ME!

Panel 5: ** Me hanging out with the gf one night.

Panel 6: "Hey I got some xanax from a friend. Wanna take one?"
"yeah, okay ill take one."

Panel 7: TWENTY MINUTES LATER

Panel 8: "Well this is pretty awesome.. ...sexytimes??"
"...sexytimes."

121.

*Gf reaches for pillow to muffle her sexytime noises
*After a few minutes the moans turn into growls, I jump on board and growl back.
"GRRRRRRR"
"Gr..rrr.rr"
*Suddenly the pillow falls off her face.
"Zzzzzz ZzzZzZZ zZZzzzZ"
Those were snores not growls!!
Did I just date-rape my Girlfriend??!?!?

What women think men do during long showers
FAP
FAP
FAP
FAP
What men really do in the shower
Le click of secret button
Le secret door

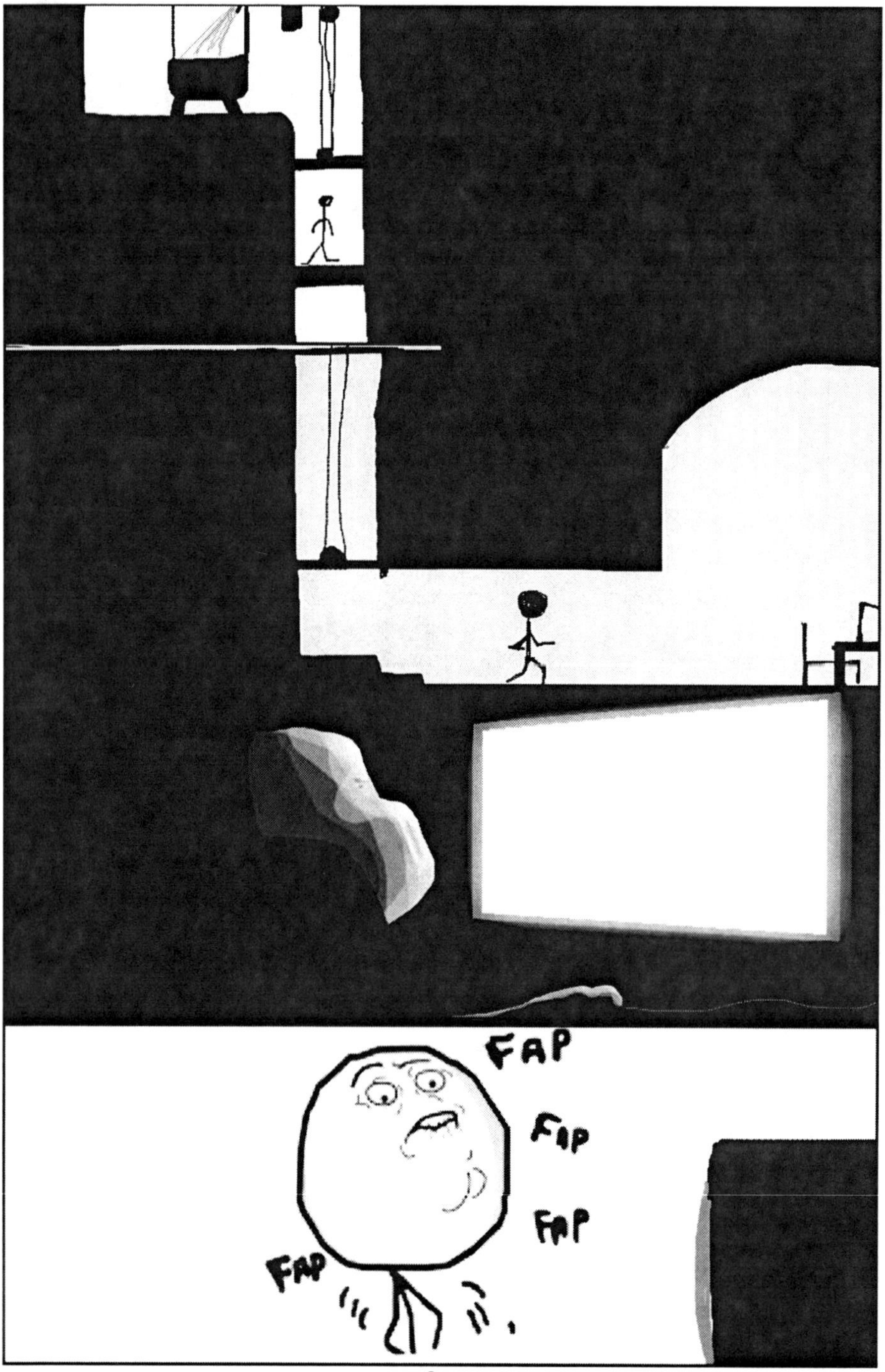
FAP
FAP
FAP
FAP

me, meeting someone new for the first time

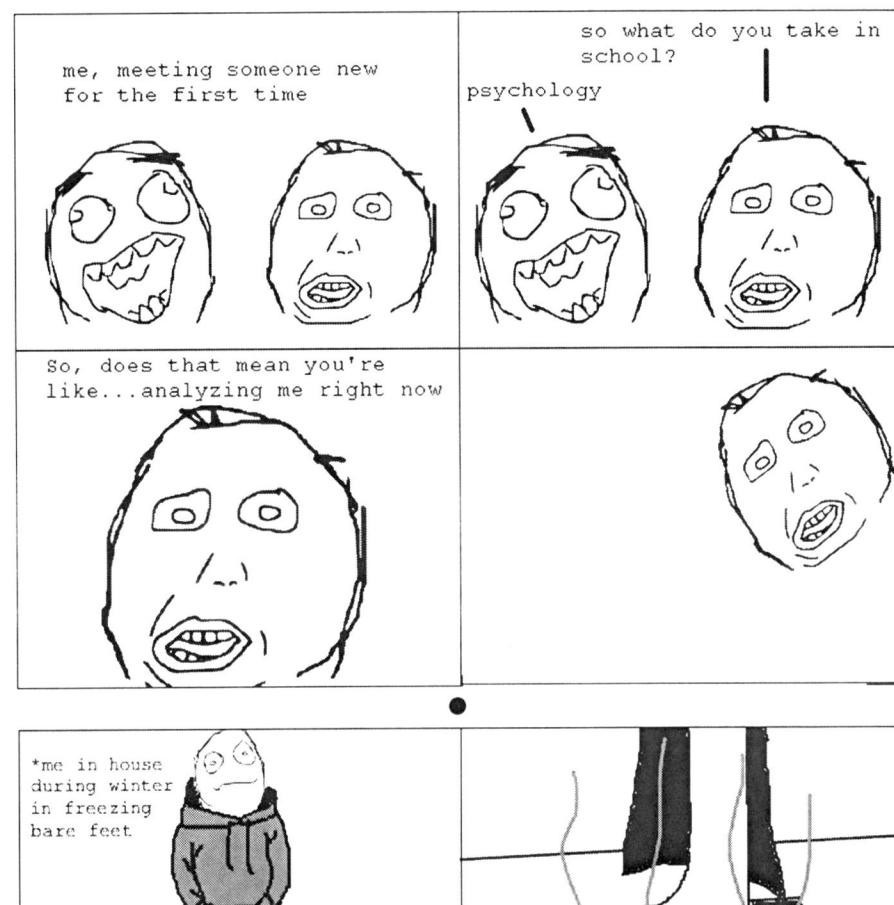

so what do you take in school?
psychology

So, does that mean you're like...analyzing me right now

*me in house during winter in freezing bare feet

*poorly drawn baggy pants

*put foot on floor vent

*poof!

Oh, sweet jesus

125.

Me, going to awesome girl's house for first time to watch a movie. *The goddess in question*	We go to the garage/entertainment room
Pretty impressed by the sight, I observe my environment. Hey I like what you've done out here!	Thanks! Go ahead and take a seat on the couch and I'll get the movie going!
I notice something... Is that a...	It is!!!

126.

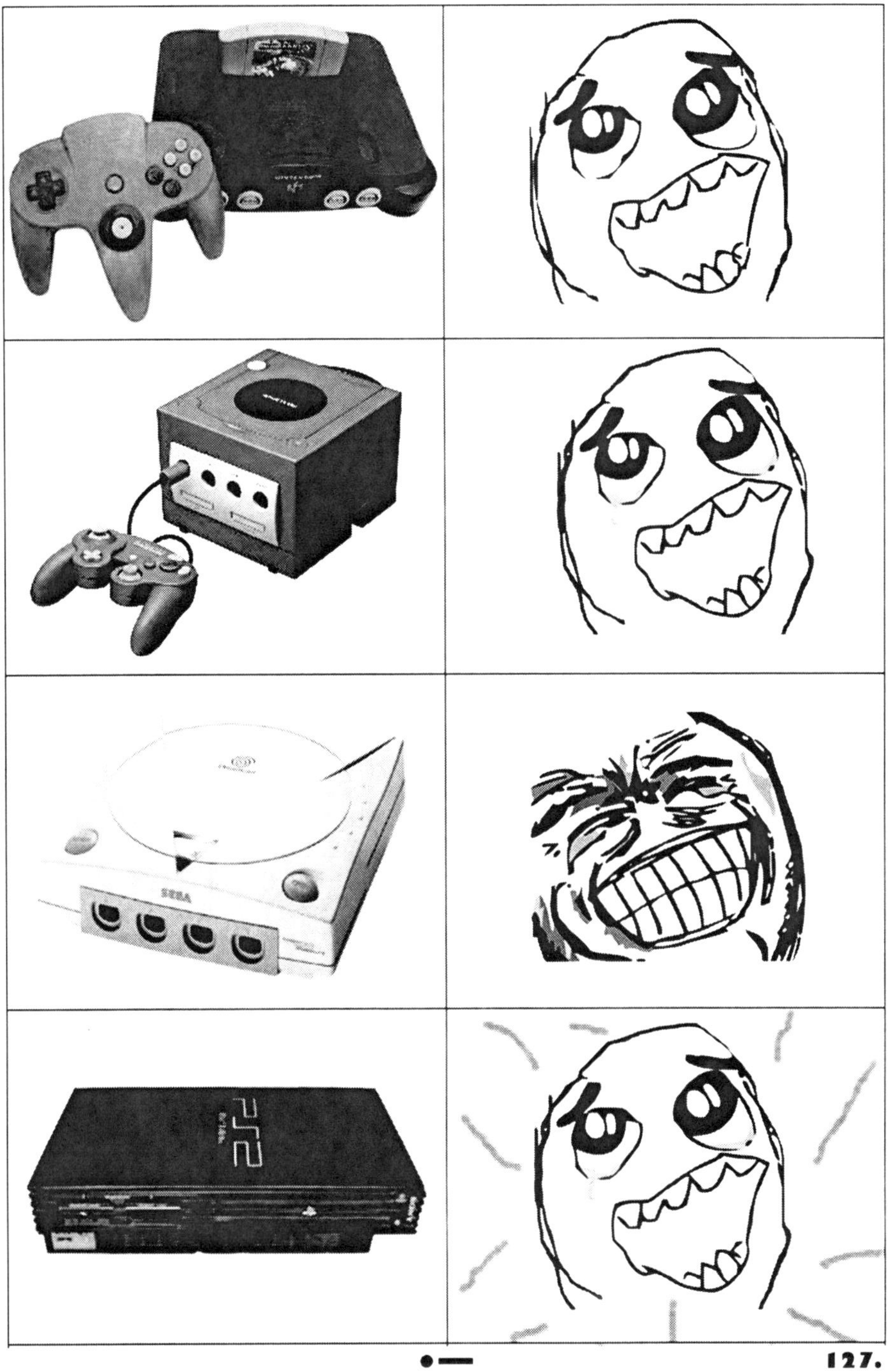
SEGA

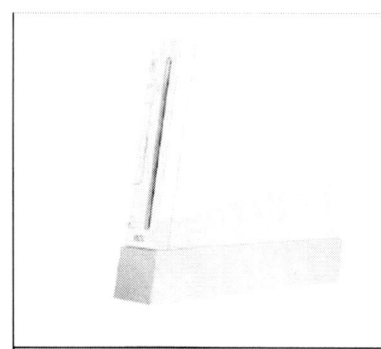

My fair maiden, my shining paragon of all that is good and beautiful in this world, I, Derp, do solemnly pledge to thee on this, the 6th day of the 11th month of the 11th year of the 21st century, to take you as my bride. I shall never forsake this oath, and it shall bind me 'til thy love accept me, or death take me.

* le me going to go see a movie with le gf

Hey it's my turn to pick the movie! Lets go see the Time Traveller's Wife!

Awesome baby! I'm so excited!
Okay
* Me watching the movie crying like a bitch. Fuck you don't judge me.
TWO HOURS LATER...
*After the movie I go to the bathroom with red eyes from crying. Random bro appears.
*Dammnn Brah! Your eyes are red as hell you must have been smokin some good shit!
*Wha? Um Yeah brah You know it
*Me non smoker
*You got any to share brah?
*Aw nah brah sorry dawg I smoked it all
*Dang brah. No prob dawg keeps it reals.
*uh yeah you too brah.
I CRIED!!!

*le me, just getting out of the bath	We're currently having renovations done in our bathroom and there's a massive hole in the floor. This means that you can see down into the kitchen if you're using the toilet or bath. (*le hole)
Knowing that I was alone in the house, I swung one leg across to retrieve a towel.	And I was quite happy...
... Until I looked down.	*Older brother's friend, staring up at me in horror.

WHO THE FUCK LET YOU IN?

Me trying to sleep as I have an exam tomorrow
Sup brah, stay awake with me
In that case, I hope you like "Establishment and use of reference values"

Das Me, at work as a waitress, doing my grad school homework like a $2.15 an hour beerwench
I have ~30 pages of writing and over two hundred of reading to get done in 4 days. Also three full shifts at work.

Suddenly, a wild table appears!

Hi there! I'm derpie and I'll be taking care of y'all this afternoon. Can I start ya with something to drink?

EVERY.
SINGLE.
PERSON.
AT.
THE.
TABLE.

"somethin' to drink?
"huh? oh, water"

"can I get you a drink?"
"what? oh, iced tea"

"somethin' to drink?"
"what? oh, water"

"anything for you, hon?"
"what? oh, water"

*In my head

*What they saw

I continue being the happiest, most helpful gorram waitress ever

I approach them with their perfectly drawn lunches

LATER

And I begin dealing them out to their recipients	Customer is happy to see his food arrive, and sees how full my hands are. "Here, lemme make that easier on you!" and proceeds to help me pass plates out
His friend: "pfft, don't help her. Her life is easy enough"	"...easy enough" "easy enough..."

"HOW DARE YOU MAKE ASSUMPTIONS ABOUT MY LI... RIVELAGED FUCKING ... SOME OF US HAVE ... TO SCHOOL ... HOLES LIKE ... R SCHOOL SO I CA... PAYS ME MORE ... AN HOUR"

FFFFFFF
FFFFFF
FFF
FUU
UUU
UUU
UUU
UUUU
UUUU-

"Here's your salad..."

I AM THE
CREATOR   OF THE WAVES

*Me working at Mega Derp Exchange, a store that buys/sells cds, movies, video games, and systems.

*A wild customer appears with at least 3 copies of each of these games. Some

134.

Hey can I sell these here? I beat them and got sick of playing them.
*All the games are still factory sealed by the way, never opened.
"These just came out in the past two weeks how could you have bea-"
"I got them for my birthday, everyone ended up getting me the same thing!"
actual quote
"Whatever you say...Let me just check these into our system. Can I see a driver's license?"
Just then...
My boss called me in back to tell me that Target reported theft of some new video games which match the same ones this guy was selling to us so....
*I distract this guy while my boss calls the cops.
"If you want to look around for a bit my boss has to get money from the safe for you."
*Five Minutes Later
"Yeah dood I think he's going to buy them...etc..ha ha yeah brah...etc..."
Enter: Sweet Justice
"Boy, you better hang that phone up and come with me, I got some questions for ya."
"Maaaannn..... dood I gotta call you back, this guy decided to be a retard and call the cops..."

*He tried running but got tackled in the parking lot. I scanned his ID and now he's forever banned.

*Made this comic at work while waiting for the cops too.

GTFO

Me, trying to log into an online account.

Error: Not a valid password.

"Hmm... maybe it's one of my old passwords..."

Error: Not a valid password.

"Guess it's not this one..."

Error: Not a valid password.

"Or that one..."

Error: Not a valid password.

"Or that one..."

136.

ONE MINUTE THIRTY SEVEN SECONDS LATER...

Error: Not a valid password.

"WHY WON'T YOU WORK?!@#@?!?"

After trying everything I've ever used as a password I attempt one more try...

"Hooray!! I'm so glad I finally got in! I can't believe I forgot that the password was..."

"...that it was..."

"umm..."

Fuck.

137.

*Me in Astronomy class learning about Stars

Professor

This star right here is called Betelgeuse (pronounced like beetle juice)....

...stars were named by the Arabs, "Betelgeuse" means armpit in old Arabic.

...and the second brightest star in orion is Betelgeuse

Driving my Jetta like a boss
Suddenly I spot an unidentified creature slowly making its way up the passenger seat
FUCKING DINOSAUR BUG
(Didn't know what it was at the time)
On the highway, I can't stop. So I just try my hardest not to wreck while making sure the bastard doesn't attack.
It stops on the headrest...
I roll down the back window...
*bzzzk
(press)
BACKHAND, BITCH!
WHAP
FUCK YEA.

*le young me at friend's house, playing
friend
me
hey Derp, you hungry?
yeah I could go for a snack!
Moooom! Derp's hungry!!!

Professor: This class is going to take a lot of work, attendance is mandatory, and the tests will be based off of the readings.
*half of the fucking class
*me
Man this really sucks but I need this class so I'm gonna suck it up. At least he's being fair telling us up front.
Professor: Now that we got all the lazy people out of here, let's have an easy semester.
NOT BAD

Me just hanging out, when all of a sudden my phone rings.
Seeing that it's my bank, I answer the phone and say hello.
An automated voice answers.
"Hello, this is an important message from herpderp bank."
"Please hold while an agent is reached to speak with you."
After holding for about five minutes...
"An agent could not be reached to speak with you."
"We will call back later, or we can be reached at herpderp bank's customer service line."
Hangs up on me
IF YOU WEREN'T AVAILABLE TO TALK TO ME THEN WHY THE FUCK DID YOU CALL!?

$1,000
Yay tax return! I'll be able to build myself a new PC for the first time in 5 years!
- $600
Hi dear, I just quit my job so I'll need you to pay my part of the rent for this month
Okay
- $250
And my bills and insurance.
Okay
-$145
And all our groceries.
Okay
$5
Well, I still have enough left to spend a little bit on myself.
yay
BICYCLE
Look what I got! Want to play some cards?
No.
BICYCLE
okay
BICYCLE

There's only Sky Mall to read on this plane? Who buys that crazy junk anyway?	I suppose I'll flip through it once and then sleep...
	5 DAYS LATER

143.

Me, selling fish like a boss
A CUSTOMER APPROACHES
WHY IS IT THAT ALL YOUR FISH IS FROM OTHER COUNTRIES I ONLY BUY FROM THE US I WONT EAT ANYTHING FROM CHINA HOW COME YOU DONT BUY AMERICAN DO YOU WANT FORIEGNERS STEALING ALL OF OUT JOBS WHY DONT YOU HAVE AMERICAN FISH FROM AMERICA FOR AMERICANS?
I mean, look at this one, "Chilean Sea Bass" Where the hell is that from?
...Chile... South America...
FINALLY! What part of South America is Chile in? Like Texas or Louisiana or something?

DON'T DIE MY LOVE...
DON'T WORRY, I BELEIVE IN REINCARNATION. I'll BECOME A BEAUTIFUL ANIMAL IN THE AFTERLIFE
NOOOOOOOOOO
3 SEC LATER...
YAY, I'M A FLY! REINCARNATION WORKS!
SPLAT
3 SEC LATER...
YAY I'M A BIRD!
CRUNCH
3 SEC LATER...
YAY I'M A SNAKE!

3 SEC LATER...
YAY.......
I'M A CHIMPANZEE
3 SEC LATER...
YAY I'M AN ELEPHANT
NOT AGAIN!
CRUNCH
FUCK YEA

This date is going so well! This girl is fantastic! I hope dinner is good!
So what do you feel like tonight?
I'm open to anything. I'm sure I'll find something good.

3 MINUTES LATER

Hi I'm Wanda, and I'll be your waitress tonight.

About time...

I'm sorry ma'am. I came just as soon as I could.

Bring us some appetizers, on the house.

I'll see what I can do.

Not necessary? She took her sweet time getting here!

That's not necessary, Wan-

I'll be back in a sec!

Gosh that spaghetti looks good!

She's mean to waitresses

147.

*dad hunting deer
*dad cooks the deer secretly
So kids guess what it is?
???
-Ok guys, I'm gonna give you a clue. I'ts what your mother calls me.
it's a fucking dick,dont eat it!!!!

Me, in a particularly surly mood, browsing the internet.	When out of nowhere, my cat jumps right in front of the monitor.
OHMAIGGAWD CAT YOU'RE IN THE WAY GTFO.	Wait...no... what have I done?
I'M SORRY SANDERP, COME BACK, LET ME LOVE YOU!	*Sanderp comes running, because Sanderp is awesome.*

I'm going to be a crazy cat-man when I'm older, aren't I?

*Le me
FAILING
Theology student at a pretigeous Theological College...
*My class
Training Minister
Theologian
Me
Theologian
Prof Derpingson teaching us about ancient proverbs
-nods-
Oh great merciful father in heaven why is it not lunch yet?
Hmmm, yes yes yeesss...
-nods-
Egypt blah blah wisdom blah blah
ancient blah blah proverbs blah
blah blah mumble mumble stutter
laughs at own joke
ugh blah wisdomous
h blah blah blah
Here is an example of an ancient Egyptian proverb...
SNORE
The word is a bird-
Once released no one can recapture it.
*Le well drawn projector screen
-nods-
-nods-
Hmmm, yes yes yeesss...

Why does
that sou-...
CAUSE
EVERYBODY'S
HEARD
ABOUT
THE BIRD
silence
So you
haven't
heard about
the bird?
True Story

*me waiting for my friend
at a parking-lot*
*Suddenly become aware that
I might look like shit*

A wild car window appeared!

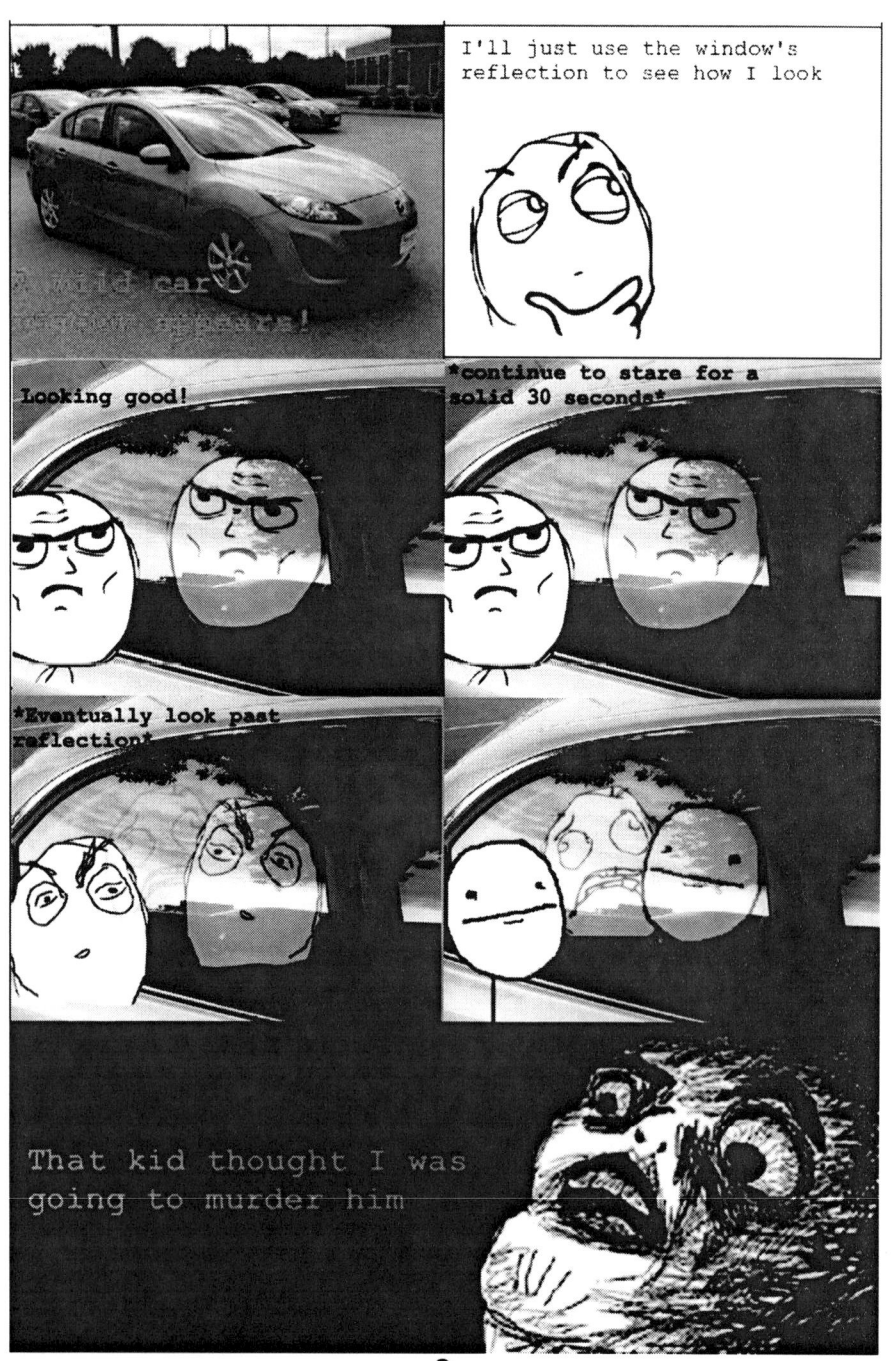

I'll just use the window's reflection to see how I look

Looking good!

continue to stare for a solid 30 seconds

Eventually look past reflection

That kid thought I was going to murder him

152.

I met a cool guy and I'm gonna spend the night at his place. Don't worry I won't cheat! Okay	*Le cheat*
Thanks for all the gifts and really expensive sushi but I'm leaving you. Problem?	le text Alex: *suicidal thoughts*
Alex: NOT ON MY WATCH	

To Alex and every friend who's there when you need it:

Thank you.

le me, sophomore, heading to first class of the semester

When Suddenly, wild freshmen appear

"Excuse me sir, could you help me find The acaderp building"

"Sure follow me"

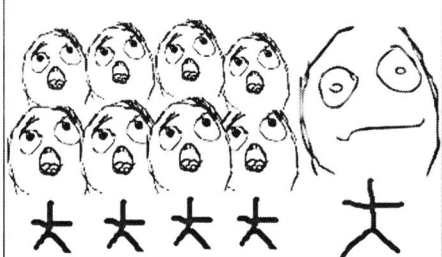

"Herp, you need to talk more. You've cooked here for 2 years and no one knows you..."

"Herp, you literally have no emotion.

What's wrong with you?"

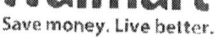

"Herp, you're the worst greeter we've ever seen. You haven't spoken to one customer the entire time you've been here..."

I've never been so scared in my entire life...

"ALL YOU BITCHES NEED TO START ACTING MORE LIKE PTE. HERP! HE IS ONE STONEFACED, BADASS, COLD BLOODED KILLER.

HELL I'D BE SCARED TO GO UP AGAINT HIM IN COMBAT! SHAPE UP YOU PATHETIC MAGGOTS!!!"

Me, a deaf guy who wears a cochlear implant
8:01 PM
Me and a couple friends hanging out
Me
Friend1
Friend2
Dude, some guy at work told me that this prostitute he got with in Vegas was like riding an elephant. The fuck?!
(What my friend really said)
...riding elephants...
(What I heard)
Dude, what's the big deal? I've ridden a couple....
What?
.....
Me
Friend1
Friend2
Are you saying you got with some hookers?
Friend 1

What? What the hell are you talking about? I'm talking about some damn elephants.
Me
You just said you've ridden a couple of hookers.
Friend 1
(apparently forgetting that he mentioned elephants)
Dude, I was talking about elephants. How did hookers even come into this?
Me
Were you not listening?? Are you deaf or something??
Friend 1 - Still very forgetful
Friend 2
Me
Friend 1, realizing his snafu
Me
Friend1
Friend2

me on payday

that night, after paying bills

I will suck your dick for chicken nugs

Ok, Time to go home.

Later!

As i am walking out the door

Bites my shirt tail not wanting me to leave

It is ok. I will be back later.

Bark Bark Bark Bark

I miss you too

157.

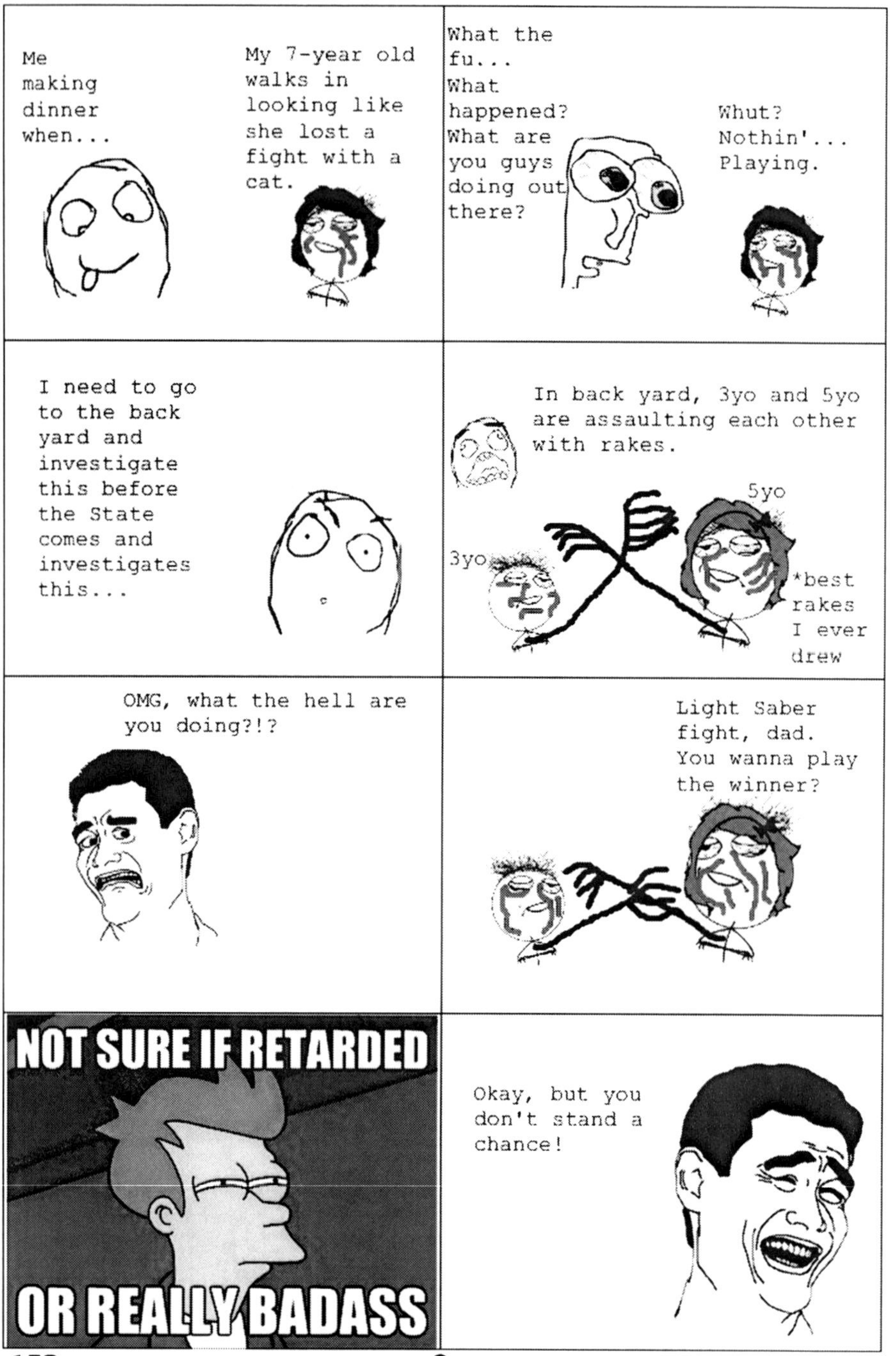
Me making dinner when...
My 7-year old walks in looking like she lost a fight with a cat.
What the fu... What happened? What are you guys doing out there?
Whut? Nothin'... Playing.
I need to go to the back yard and investigate this before the State comes and investigates this...
In back yard, 3yo and 5yo are assaulting each other with rakes.
5yo
3yo
*best rakes I ever drew
OMG, what the hell are you doing?!?
Light Saber fight, dad. You wanna play the winner?
NOT SURE IF RETARDED
OR REALLY BADASS
Okay, but you don't stand a chance!

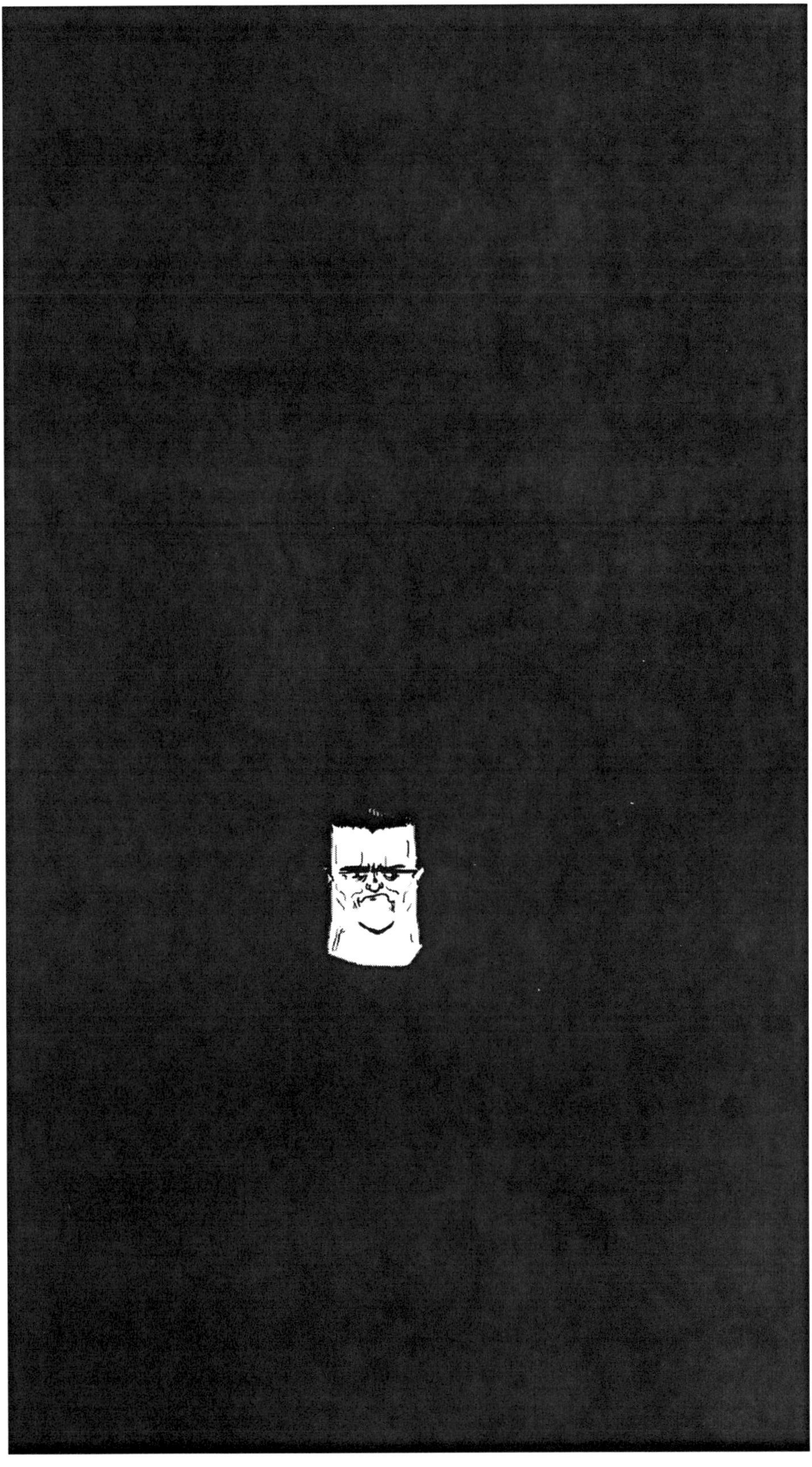

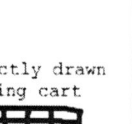

Me in the grocery store, tired after a long day's work. *Perfectly drawn shopping cart*	I could use a drink when I get home!
	Hmm.. What should I get?
Bacardi is good! I'll take a bottle. Now I just need something to mix it with.	I don't know any drinks. Maybe there's a recipe on that Bacardi poster over there.
BACARDI TOGETHER — JUST ADD FRIENDS — BACARDI SUPERIOR	

Me, a deaf guy who wears a cochlear implant.
This series will depict a few of my experiences...
3:28 AM
Me and my woman asleep when...
(I can't hear when sleeping as I take my device off)
CREAK!
Baby! Wake up! I think someone is in the house!
Ssssnnnnrrrrkkkk! Whuh? I can't see your mouth.
What my wife thinks I see:
Will you check the house? I heard a noise!
What I actually see:

It's too dark to read your lips! You want me to rock your house? Wha-?	No, baby! I heard a noise! Please check the house!
You need my boys? I'm so confused...this is a dream, right? I'm dreaming....	No, baby...I just thought someone broke in.
Oh! I love you, too!	
me, sitting outside smoking.	when suddenly I see my friends truck coming up the road with some people in the back

162.

le brilliant idea - i'll go jump in his truck when he gets to the stop sign!

CHALLENGE ACCEPTED

Beautiful running leap into back

What I see...

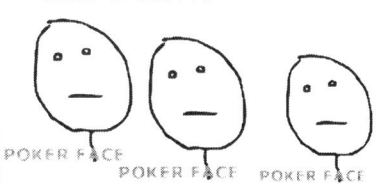

POKER FACE   POKER FACE   POKER FACE

me: hey, sorry.. uh.. so..where you guys headed

Girlfriend and I talking
Do you remember my friend Diana?
How could I forget her?! Me and her would always go to her basement after school and...
And what?!
fuck fuck fuck fuck fuck
HMMMM?!!!!

PUT THAT FUCKING CANDY AWAY!!!

FFFFFFF
FFFFFF
FFFFF
FFFUU
UUU
UU
UUUU
UUUU-

Okay

me, an italian 20 years old exchange student in the USA

IN FEBRUARY

damn, i can't believe i still can't purchase alcohol in this country.

wait a sec. i was born on december 1st, that means that on my italian ID, the date is 1/12

american people might actually believe that i was born in january 12th here, therefore being 21.

165.

hi, may i see your ID please?

yes, it's an european ID, I hope it is ok

sure just show me the birthdate

BAD POKER FACE

LIQUOR STORE

You died on a Saturday...

We found you with a baby carrot in your mouth. They were your favorite.

166.

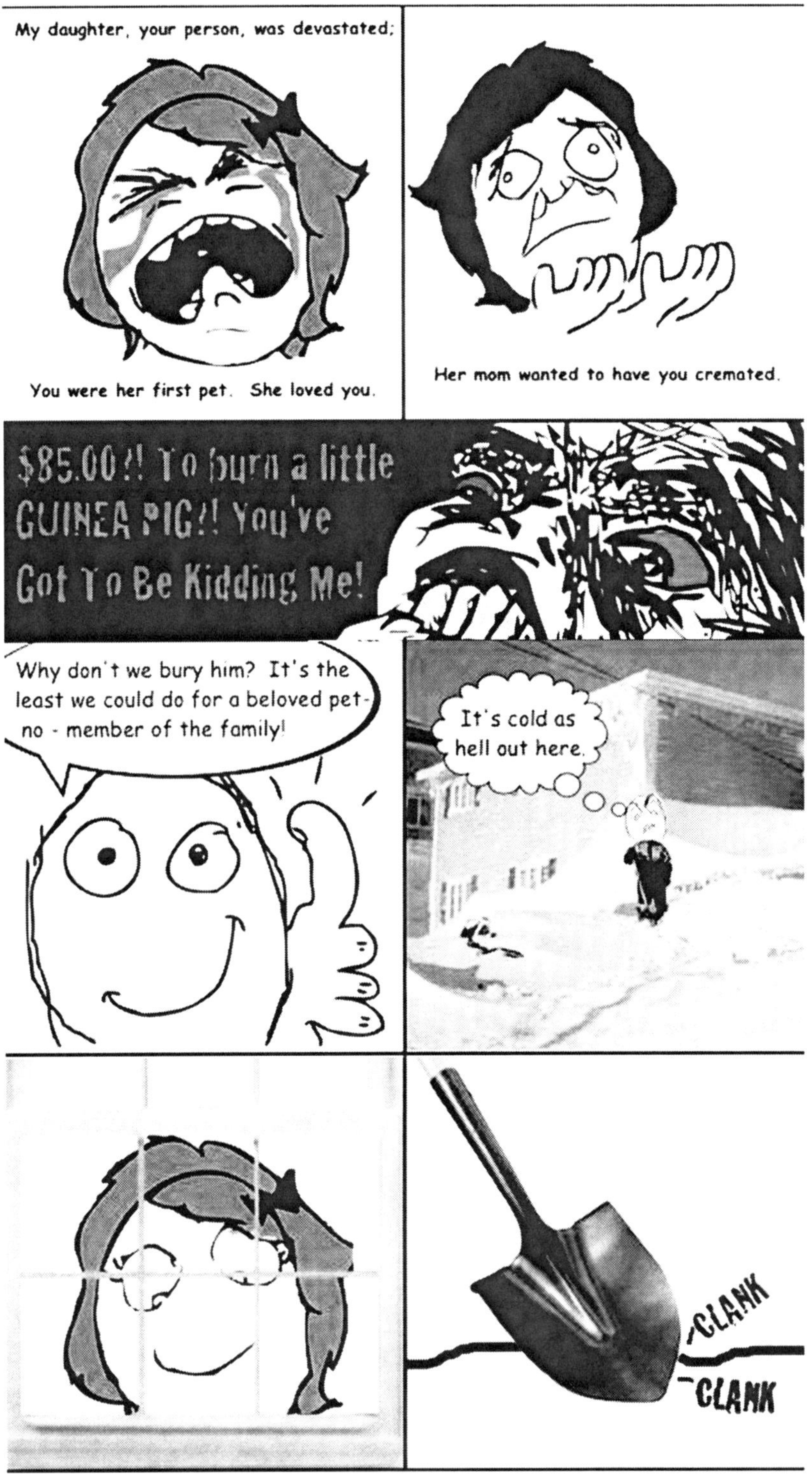

My daughter, your person, was devastated;
You were her first pet. She loved you.
Her mom wanted to have you cremated.
$85.00?! To burn a little GUINEA PIG?! You've Got To Be Kidding Me!
Why don't we bury him? It's the least we could do for a beloved pet- no - member of the family!
It's cold as hell out here.
CLANK
CLANK

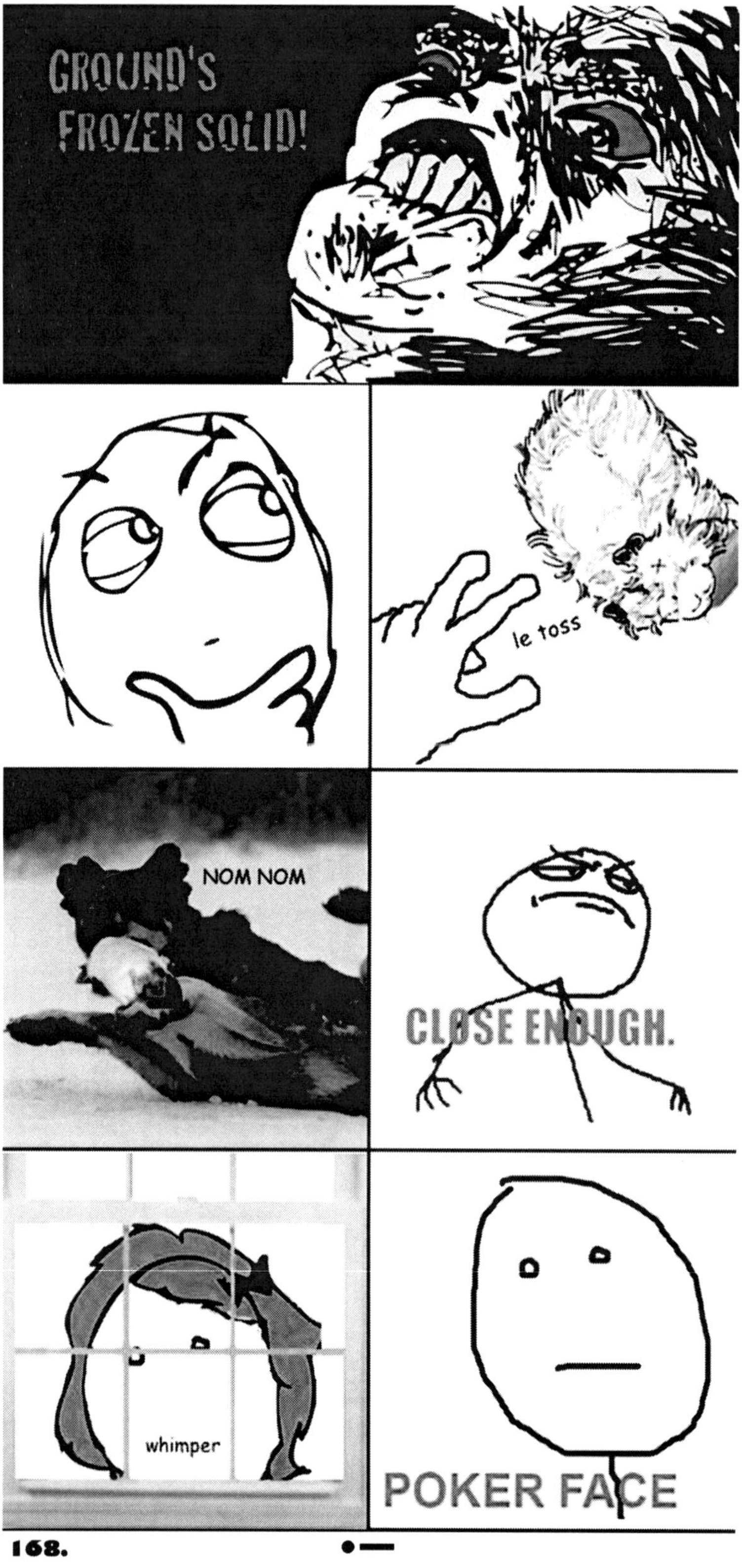
GROUND'S FROZEN SOLID!
le toss
NOM NOM
CLOSE ENOUGH.
whimper
POKER FACE

Dr. H. Derp
Child Pyschologist
$80.00 for a psychologist visit?!
$85.00 (cremation)
- $80.00 (pyschologist)
$5.00 Cost Savings
EVERYTHING WENT BETTER THAN EXPECTED

schlick schlick
Schlick schlick
Schlick schlick
Schlick schlick
Schlick
schlick schlick
schlick schlick

HOW TO WIN THE LOTTERY

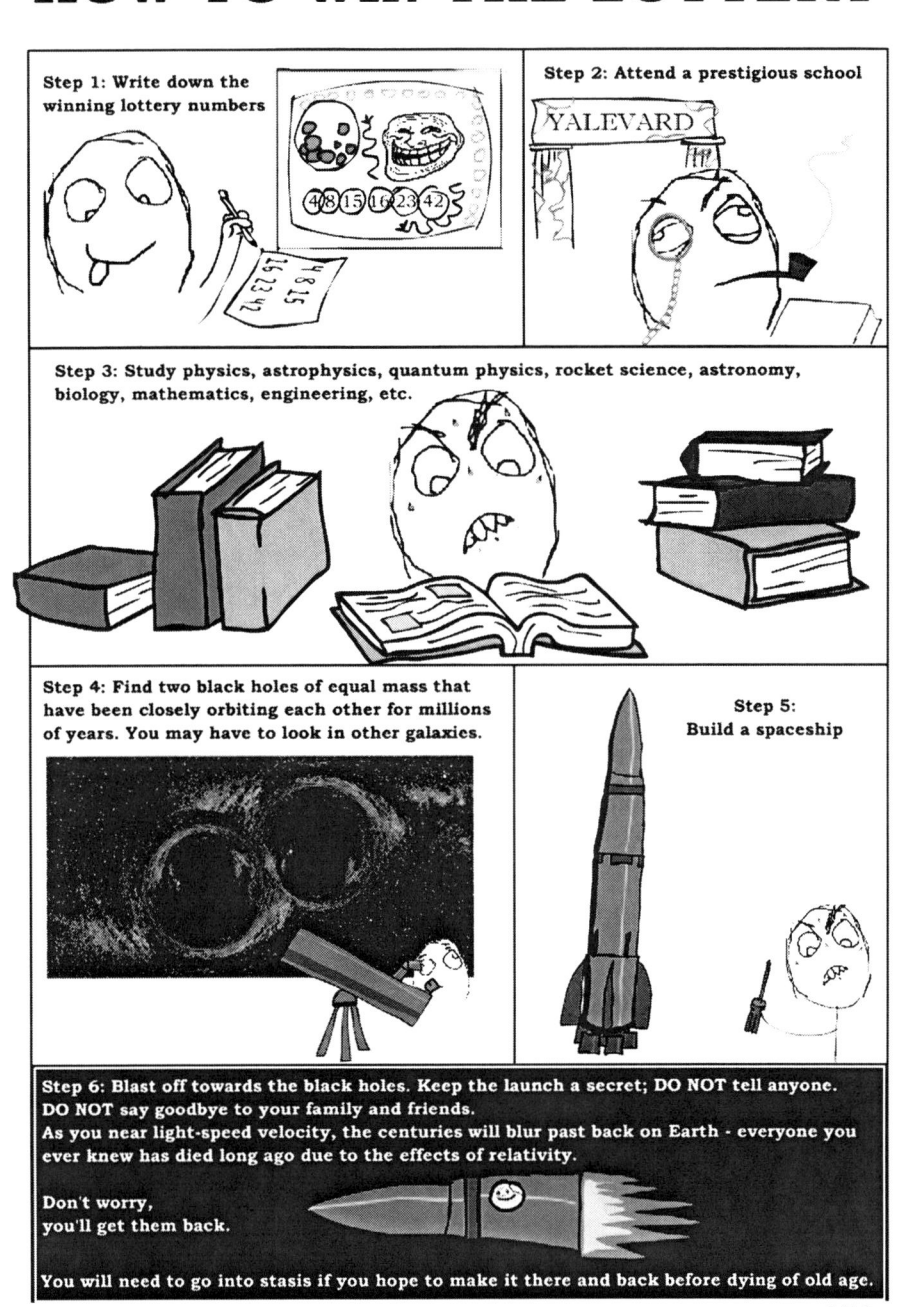

Step 1: Write down the winning lottery numbers

Step 2: Attend a prestigious school

Step 3: Study physics, astrophysics, quantum physics, rocket science, astronomy, biology, mathematics, engineering, etc.

Step 4: Find two black holes of equal mass that have been closely orbiting each other for millions of years. You may have to look in other galaxies.

Step 5: Build a spaceship

Step 6: Blast off towards the black holes. Keep the launch a secret; DO NOT tell anyone. DO NOT say goodbye to your family and friends.
As you near light-speed velocity, the centuries will blur past back on Earth - everyone you ever knew has died long ago due to the effects of relativity.

Don't worry,
you'll get them back.

You will need to go into stasis if you hope to make it there and back before dying of old age.

Step 7: As you arrive at your destination, do some math and pilot the ship into a *closed timelike curve* around the black holes. You are now traveling backwards through time. DO NOT allow yourself to crash into yourself. DO NOT enter the event horizons.

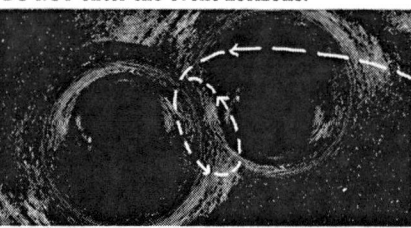

Step 8: Go back into stasis. You will need to orbit the black holes for a very long time. You need to compensate for the time it took you to get there, the time it will take you to get back to Earth, plus the many years which have passed since you wrote down the winning lottery numbers.

Step 9: When the time is right, power up the engines and break free from the black holes. DO NOT crash into yourself during the transition. Point yourself towards Earth and re-enter stasis.

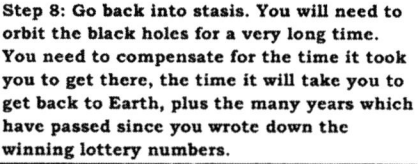

Step 10: Return to Earth. You must arrive and purchase the winning ticket before the numbers are drawn.

YOU ARE NOT DONE YET.

Step 11: NO ONE MUST KNOW ANYTHING. You must remain in hiding - otherwise, you could cause paradoxes involving your past self, who willan be on-studyen at a prestigious school.

Step 12: DO NOT sign the ticket. Make photocopies of the ticket and stash the original somewhere safe.

Step 13: Lawyer up. Form an LLC and give it ownership of the ticket. Use the LLC to claim your winnings, and then transfer the funds to yourself.

Step 14: Ensure that the money is invested at a low risk so that it will earn enough interest to overcome inflation.

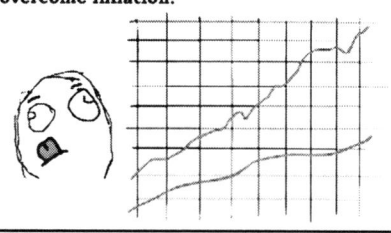

Step 15: In order to avoid paradoxes, return to your spaceship, which should be well hidden, and re-enter stasis for the last time.

Step 16: You can exit stasis in a few years, once your past self has built their spaceship and launched it.

Step 17: You may now live out your life however you wish, with no further risk of paradoxes.

AWWW YEAH WON THE LOTTERY

typical day of fappin and browsing reddit

this is so offensive

MUST SHARE WITH EVERYONE

LOL

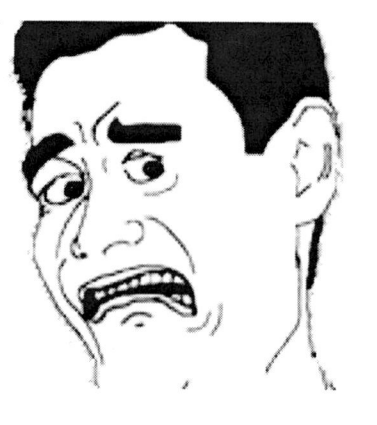

should I send to gf? she might take offense her feelings might...	*le click
few min later, fb reply from gf Derpina Derpiton April 27 at 2:44pm Report hahhaaa oh my goodness. speaking of, have you seen this? http://i69.photobucket.com/albums/i63/bkusler/i-love-you-this-much.png i69.photobucket.com	what the fu... *le click

174.

Playing ball in the park
on a sunday afternoon
Derpette, 6yo
me, mid-twenty
What are you doing with
that little kid?
We're playing. She's
my daughter.
sigh
STOP LYING! YOU'RE MOLESTING HER!
Ignore her kiddo, she got up on
the wrong side this morning.
feeling slightly pissed
STOP IGNORING ME! I'M
CALLING THE COPS!
Derpette, go get
yourself some ice
cream over there.
hands over money
She's my child.
Accept it and leave
us alone.
HERP RAGE DERP
Is he your father?
Of course, he's my
father! Best daddy
in the world.
She says it. But it was good,
that you called us. Possible
perpetrator, blah blah.

Good for what? So my taxes get thrown out of the window?

Any man playing with a child may be a pedophile. But that is not the case here, so goodbye and thank you for your cooperation.

And I am like:

WOMYN

Y U NO USE BRAIN?

*Girlfriend and me in a Voodoo-Exhibition

Interesting shit!

*Me looking at some Voodoo-Mirrors

176.

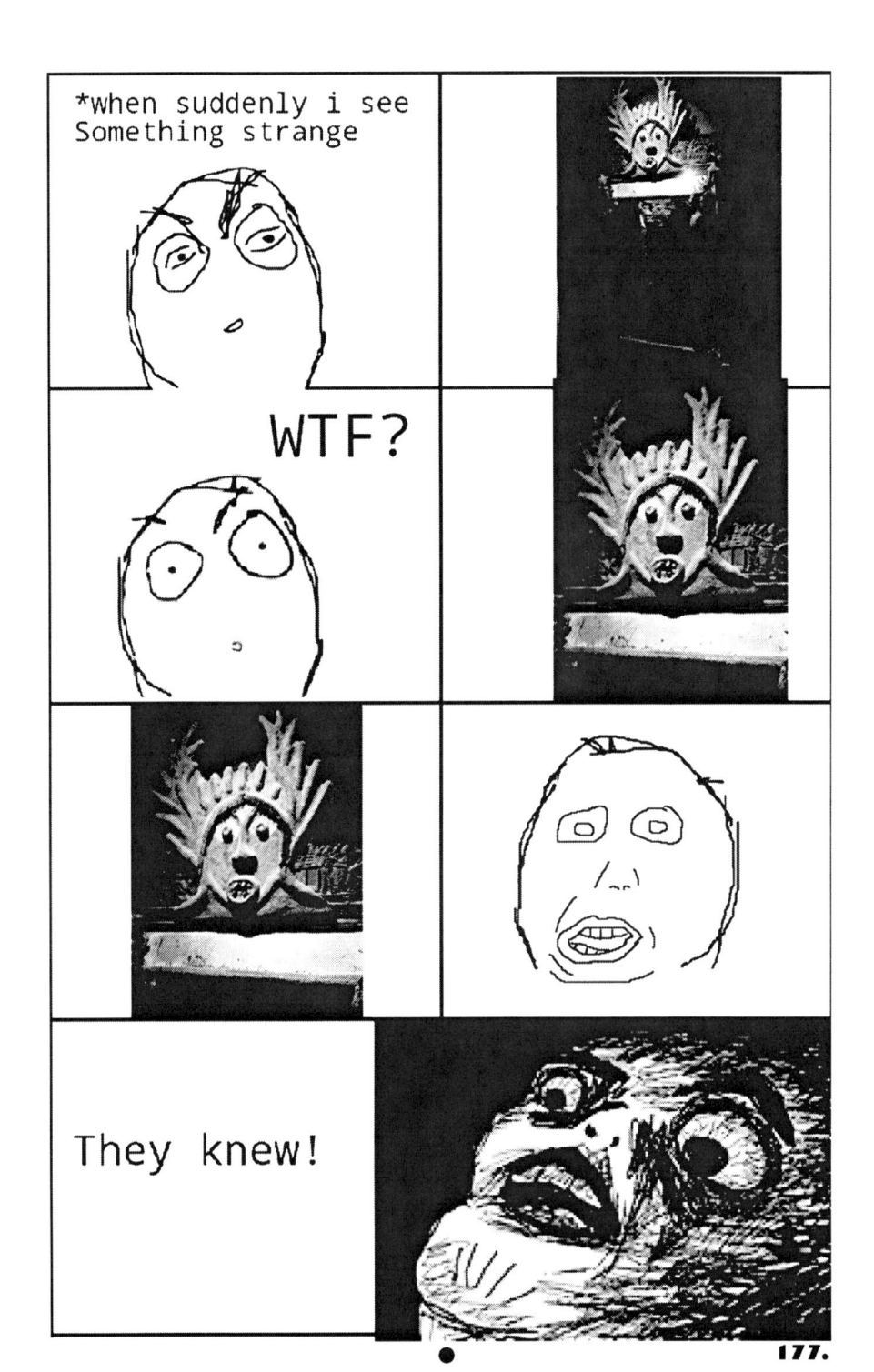

*when suddenly i see Something strange

WTF?

They knew!

*me
cashiering at derpmart like a minimum wage peon
just one more paycheck and I can get skyrim..
When suddenly a wild overweight spoiled brat appears and begins insulting
Hye poor fagut, ur a loser w/ no life.
I decide to not give a fuck as usual with these kinds of people
when le brat's obviously tired and annoyed by her son mother saunters over..
le sigh
alright, how much for these ones?
c'mon hurry i wanna fuckinggo home
that'll be 35 derp currency mam.
Last Name:
Date of Birth:
mm dd 19 yy
Next
When suddenly my register prompts me for this
Last Name:
Social Security Number:
Date of Birth:
Next
btw mam, this game has an M rating for extreme sexual content such as picking up prostitutes and going into strip clubs. I personally think it should be banned in all stores because of the adverse effects it has on children throughout their lives. It's proven that 9/10 kids who play these games develop aggressive tendancies. The other game caused a teenager to muder his family because an ingame character told him it was a mission.

JESUS
SH US
IS
NEVER PLAY THESE
IS DONE FOREVER
TAKING YOU TO
ARE THERE ANY OTHER GAMES I SHOULD WATCH OUT FOR?!
Oh yes mam, games like call of duty, gears of war, oblivion, saints row, street fighter are all proven to cut cognitive skills in children by over 75%
In fact, the xbox 360 was originall intended as a 17+ system as evident by most of the games on it. I'd never let my child near one.
Thank you very much sir. He'll never be able to get on one of those horrible mind numbers ever again.
no problem mam.
FFFFFFF
FFFFFF
FFFUU
UUUU
UUUU
UUUU
UUUU-
HAVE A NICE LIFE BITCH

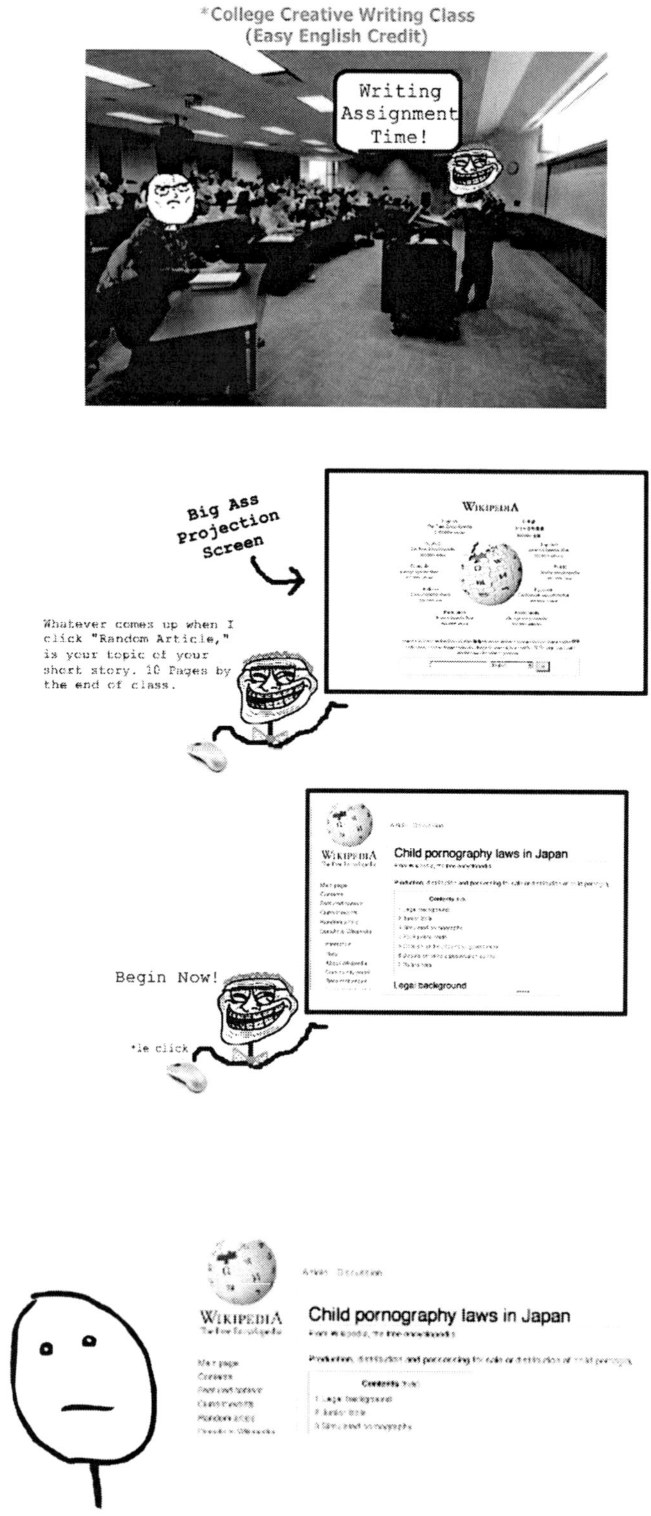
*College Creative Writing Class
(Easy English Credit)
Writing Assignment Time!
Big Ass Projection Screen
WIKIPEDIA
Whatever comes up when I click "Random Article," is your topic of your short story. 10 Pages by the end of class.
WIKIPEDIA
Child pornography laws in Japan
Legal background
Begin Now!
*le click
WIKIPEDIA
Child pornography laws in Japan

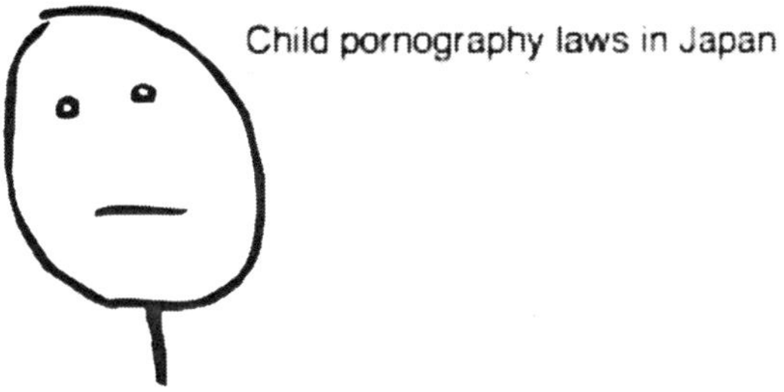
Child pornography laws in Japan

Child pornography

PROFESSOR
Y U NO CLICK AGAIN!

*Derpin around on facebook

Events

Birthdays Jessica

Hey it's Jessica's Birthday Today. I'll write on her wall.

Happy birthday

Actually, she'll get like a hundred of these....

Screw it. I'm doing this old school...

RING! RING!

Happy Birthday Jessica, long time no see... Yeah It's Derp from college... so how's life been treating you since graduation.

*Talks for an hour. She tells depressing story. Life has been shitty to her in the past year...

Hey Jessica you still live in Derptown right?

You got any birthday plans?

182.

I'm on my way...

ONE HOUR LATER

*Remembering funny stories and good times.

*Buy her an ice cream cake.

*Go out and get some drinks.

*Visit her favorite night club and dance til 2:00am

No One is Forever Alone on Their Birthday As Long As I'm Around!

183.

Me, playing on my PS2	OMG you play PS2 still - HIPSTERRRR!!
Working on my old computer	OMG why do you still use that old machine?! You must be a hipster, laaaa-loooooooool!
Listening to my 2004 era iPod	HAHA!! Not seen one of those for years, you HIPPEDY-HIP-HIPSTER!!

I'M NOT A HIPSTER - I'M JUST FUCKING POOR!!!

184.

**Bikini?
No problem**

**Underwear?
End of the world.**

On the bus to College...

Lumberjack Bearded me.

Seats.

Father & Young (6?) Son

Random Methhead tweakin' out.

"Dad, the man behind us is scary, but I'm not afraid."

"Why is that son?"

"'Cause I know the Viking in front of us will protect us."

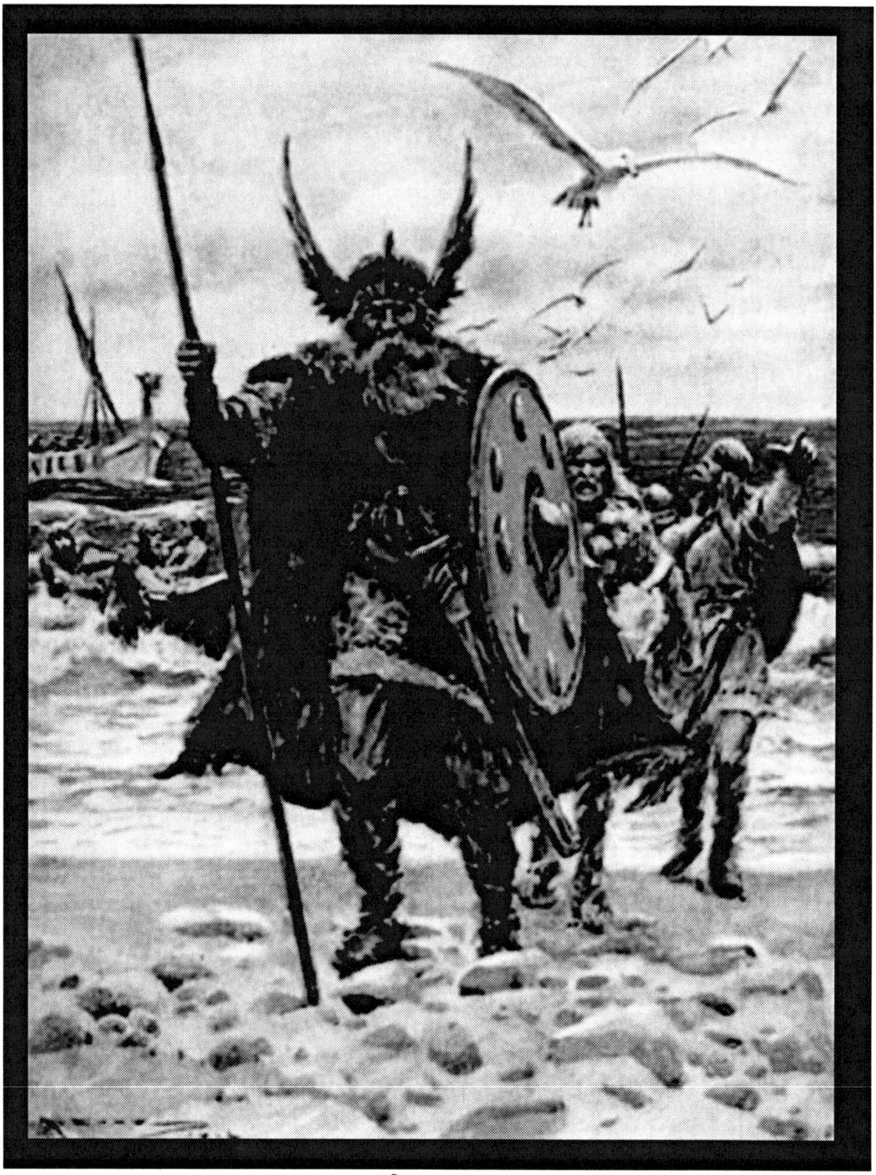

By Odin's Raven I will deliver you to safety Little Man, or I will die a Warrior's death and feast in the Halls of Valhalla until Ragnarok comes for us all.

le me watching cast away with the GF....

NOOOOOOOO WILSON!!!!!!!!!!!

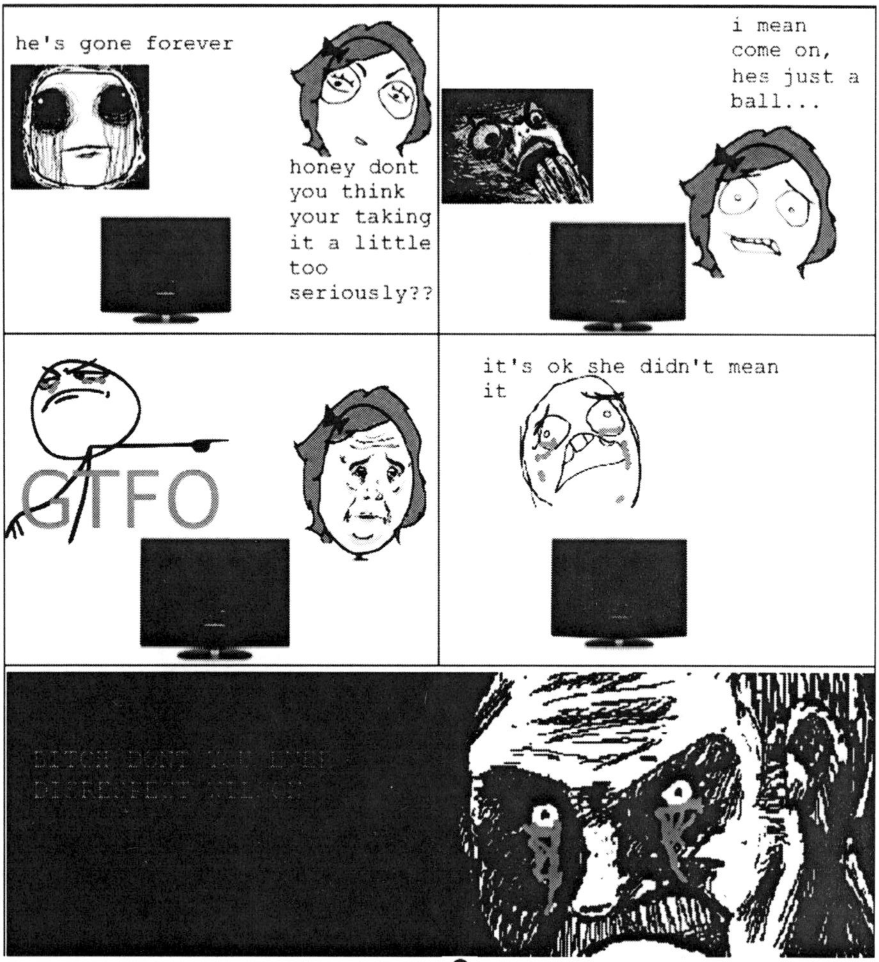
he's gone forever
honey dont you think your taking it a little too seriously??
i mean come on, hes just a ball...
GTFO
it's ok she didn't mean it

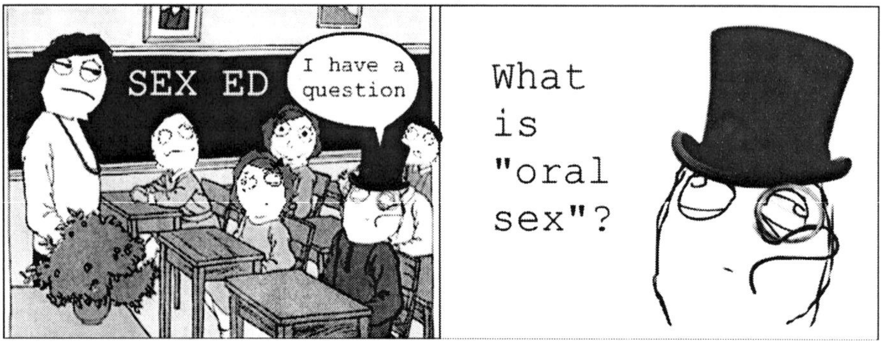
SEX ED
I have a question
What is "oral sex"?

Panel 1: Oral sex is umm.. when people umm.. talk in bed

Panel 2: LATER...

Panel 3: Do you guys want to have oral sex?

Panel 4: THE NEXT DAY

Panel 5: How was your sleepover, son? — It was great mom. We had oral sex all night long.

Panel 7: OH GOD WHY

meh have to buy new shoes and get rid of my old pair	pleeeeeaaaase don't we served you so well...
have to get a new toothbrush and get rid of my old one	pleeeaaaase don't i served you so well....
a pair of socks has a hole... have to throw them away..	pleeeaaase... don't we always held your feet warm

WHY DO ALL MY BELONGINGS HAVE A SOUL

190.

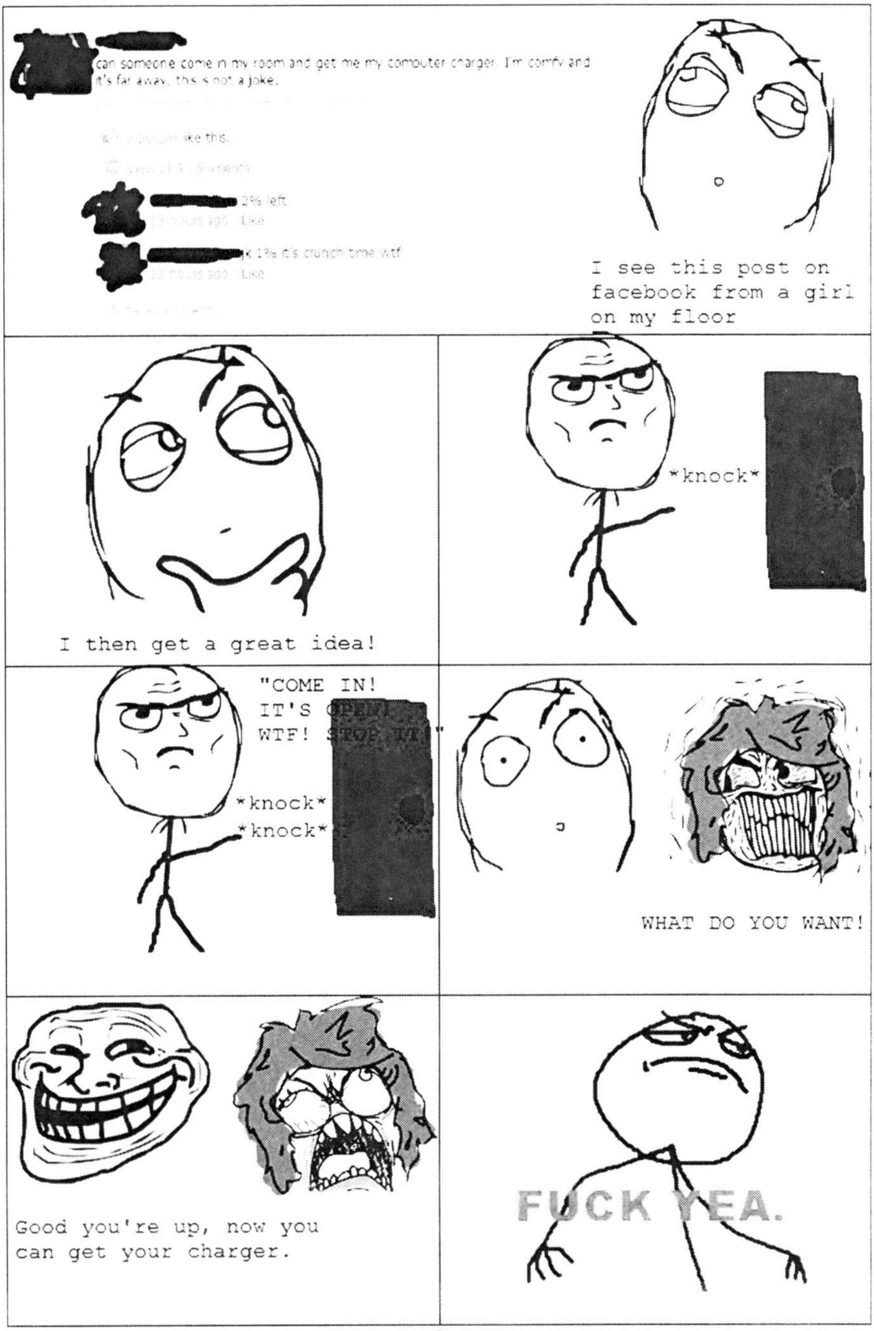

Teaching kids at school; no one paying attention
Paper starts falling
I GOT THIS SHIT
Casually toss a magnet toward the falling paper
magnet catches the paper
MID FALL
Continue walking like nothing happened
FUCK YEA.

School Supplies

Freshman

Senior

OH MY GOD SWYPE IS SO AWESOME! I'M GONNA TYPE SUPER FAST NOW!

"Hey baby! What times the movie tonight? I can't wait to see you!"

Herp bobby! What tove thy rape buttox, I count white elm to bang mom

CLOSE ENOUGH.

193.

Playing BF3 when my sister logs on *Derpette is online*	Marvelous! My sister and I shall show these ruffians what for! Tally ho!
Hey sis! I am glad you are on, I need help with this conquest map I'm on.	well stick me in a dress and call me sally! Hey there son! I would love to help you on whatever the hell it is you were talking about.
...Dad?	Thats Lt. Colonel Dad to you, asshat.
But, you don't play video games. What the hell is going on?	Well son, you play video games. I play with vaginas and tits. Your mother is gone thus my "console" is unavailable.

194.

So now with this free time I get to see what the hype is with this Xbox thing and I get to spend time with my son. A twofer indeed.	Uhh, alright. Well this is battlefield 3. It's an FPS and is pretty fast pace, but I'll cover you as best as I can.
Righto then! This sure does look pretty nice.	15 MiNuTeS LATeR...
Kills Deaths Troll Dad: 28 1 Me: 7 15	Son... Come in son, over.
Yes dad?	Orders just came down from HQ. You are to resign due to your poor performance.

195.

Turn in your dog tags and your balls to resource logistics... I have to go recieve the medal of honor and fuck your mother. Toodles!	*derpette is offline*

I was born from a god...

I got this, bro.	Straight piece thinks he's such hot shit. Psh, whatever. At least we show up on time.
I'm just happy to be here and help in any way I can!	I'm sorry I'm so fat.

Problem?

I want to aim.
Okay...
Careful now..
...Yeah...
HELICOPTER!!!
Helicopter!?!?

(At Chinese restaurant)
thx for taking
me out!
i luv u!

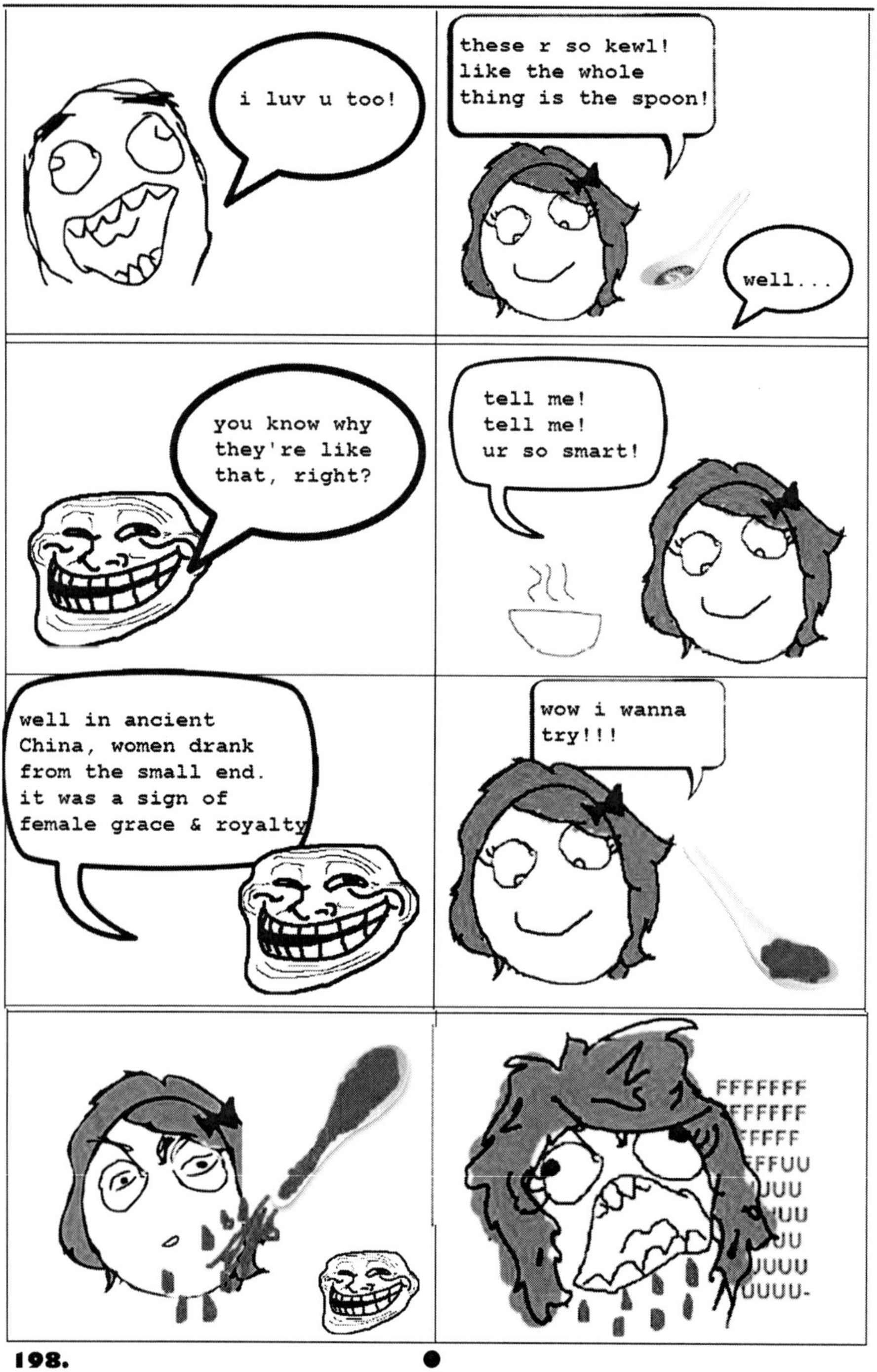
i luv u too!
these r so kewl! like the whole thing is the spoon!
well...
you know why they're like that, right?
tell me! tell me! ur so smart!
well in ancient China, women drank from the small end. it was a sign of female grace & royalty
wow i wanna try!!!
FFFFFFF FFFFFF FFFFF FFFUU UUU UUU UU UUUU UUUU-

me, a poor, starving grad student TA
Herp, can you help me outside of office hours? I can pay you
Sorry Herpina, I can't accept money from students to tutor them
Well, maybe I can pay you back in another way...?
CAFETERIA
For him as well, please

Me and my wife taking a shower
When all of a sudden she slips

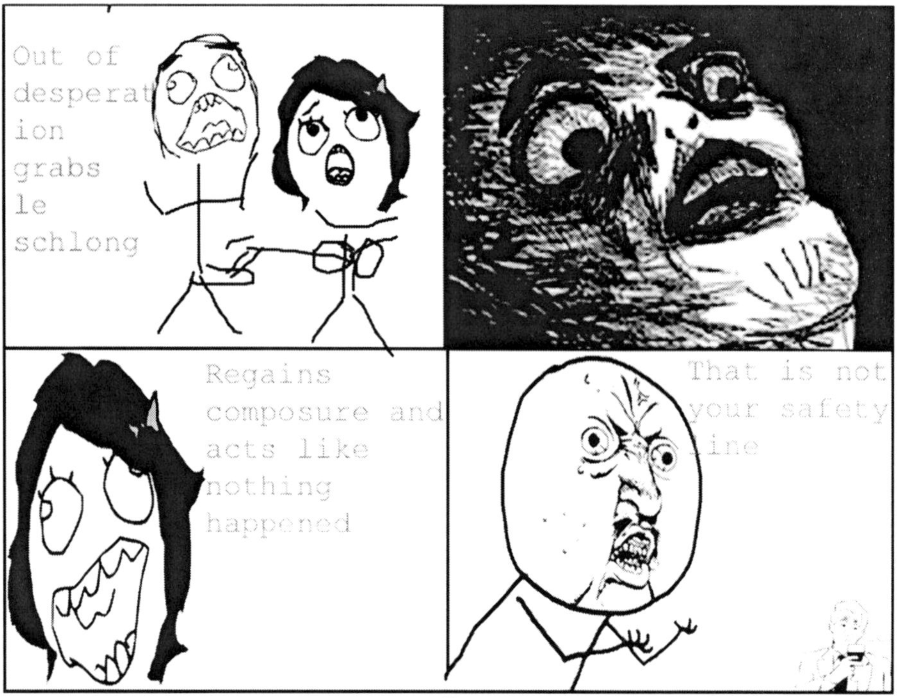
Out of desperat ion grabs le schlong
Regains composure and acts like nothing happened
That is not your safety

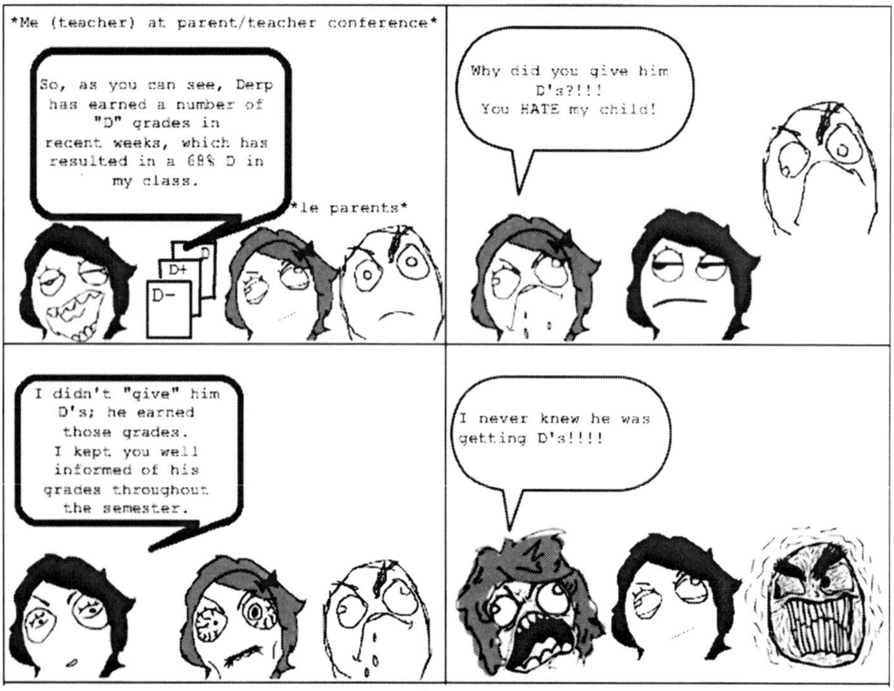
Me (teacher) at parent/teacher conference
So, as you can see, Derp has earned a number of "D" grades in recent weeks, which has resulted in a 68% D in my class.
D
D+
D-
le parents
Why did you give him D's?!!! You HATE my child!
I didn't "give" him D's; he earned those grades. I kept you well informed of his grades throughout the semester.
I never knew he was getting D's!!!!

Pulls out multiple grade notifications signed by mother
Is this your signature on all these?
Your kid has D's
Yes, but I never read those! How can you expect me to read every little piece of paper you send home?!
We're reporting you to the district!
No wonder their kid is an idiot.

~8 year old me derping around with a mechanical pencil
a wild idea appears...
puuush
i am a doctor

Us on our first date together
le nervous me
*le first GF (still dating for 2 years)
so since the game ended do you want to umm... um go somewhere like to the park?
why sure babe!
so I took her to the place right under are special tree.
Wonder what i should say to get her to kiss me
I think i got it!
???
I feel like a frog

*what i thought after that happening

WOW your so lame. I would never date a guy like you. leave now!

*what actually happened

I will make you human. Prepare yourself!

Epic first kiss!

EVERYTHING WENT BETTER THAN EXPECTED

le me working out on the arc trainer at the gym like a boss!

my 20 minutes is up

Feeling the burn!

203.

lady next to me looks down at my machine and sees my stats

"Oh look! You burnt off a cookie!"

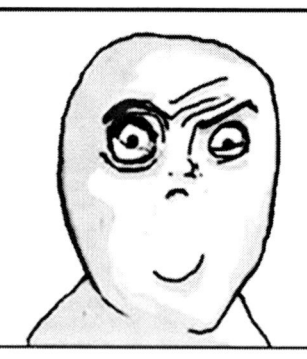

FFFFFFF
FFFFFFF
FFFFFF
FFFUU
UUUU
UUUU
UUUU
UUUU

I hope you step on a lego.

G.G.N.R.I.E.S.

204.

Think. You're smart. You can get yourself out of this

GINGERS

EVERYTHING
WENT
BETTER
THAN
EXPECTED

Hey man

They're called redheads

Yeah that shit ain't cool.

205.

Dark Rainy night at the hotel

"Front desk.."

"Can I leave my car parked under the awning over by the entrance?"

"are your windows broken on your car?"

"Of course not, I just don't want to get my car wet!"

"I'll take that as a yes? thank you!"

206.

*me walking through the shopping mall towards the exit, minding my own shit.
When suddenly, a wild, hot spanish woman approaches me with something in her hand
'Excuse me sir, would you like a free sample of our product?'
I see that she is holding a little red cube shaped thing wrapped in plastic.
'Yeah sure, i'll try what you're selling.'
I put the cube in my mouth and started munching away.
10 SECONDS LATER
'What the hell is this shit!?'
'It's soap, sir. I thought you knew. We are selling our new beauty items and are giving out free samples. Sorry lol'

'Why do you make soap thaat looks and feels like food?!!?.....................
....
....
......Give me 2 more, i'm gonna get my brother with this!'

And i did trick my brother into eating the soap and he is currently in the bathroom throwing up!

---

*le me derpin about in Spanish class

*teacher
Now before we begin, does anyone already know any spanish?

CHALLENGE ACCEPTED

*raises hand like a boss

Yes, derp!

ME GUSTA

How girls apologize:
I'm so sorry Derpina...please let's still be friends!
Let's talk about our feelings!!
Blah blah blah....
Blee blee bloo.
Jabawigjabba...?
Smootyblah...
Bleh blah blop!
Ohhhh....Okay...
How guys apologize:
Hey man...
Hey bro.
You know.
Yeah. I know.

210.●—

Let's go shopping!

Okay! I'm so glad we worked it out!

(I will hate that bitch forever, I'm going to go fuck her boyfriend now).

(What a total cunt - I'm removing her from facebook).

You catch the game last night?!! So awesome, right?!!?

I KNOW!! Let's go out for beers and play some Halo!

Hanging out with a girl I've had a crush on forever.

Me

Wanna give me a foot massage?

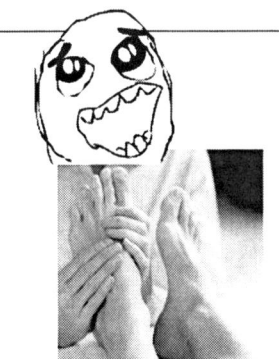

When all of a sudden, her body fucking explodes.

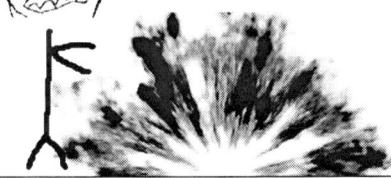

211.

I'm left holding her two severed feet.	Her severed head comes crawling towards me.
Fuck my foot.	FUCK MY FOOT OR I'LL KILL YOU!!!
Okay.	

WHAT. THE. FUCK.

212.

copyright 2011 book/design

JOIN THE COMMUNITY:
REDDIT.COM/R/F7U12

CPSIA information can be obtained at www.ICGtesting.com
Printed in the USA
LVOW121016200212

269517LV00005B/31/P